MW00475586

CHILEAN WINE

The Heritage

CHILEAN WINE

The Heritage

*A Journey from
the Origins of the Vine
to the Present*

RODRIGO ALVARADO

PROLOGUE BY
AGUSTÍN HUNEEUS

ORIGO EDICIONES • SANTIAGO, CHILE
THE WINE APPRECIATION GUILD • SAN FRANCISCO, CALIFORNIA

Chilean Wine. The Heritage
By Rodrigo Alvarado

Originally published in Chile, 2004 by
Origo Ediciones
Padre Alonso de Ovalle 748
Santiago de Chile
www.origo.cl

Editor and Publisher: Hernán Maino
Executive Editor: María José Correa
Translation: Margaret Snook
Production: Marcelo Baeza
Illustrations: Raquel Echenique

First English Edition, published 2005 by
The Wine Appreciation Guild
360 Swift Avenue
South San Francisco, CA 94080
wwww.wineappreciation.com

Copyright © Origo 2004
ISBN: 1-891267-77-9

Printed in Chile

Vineyard at the foot of Mt. Vesuvius just moments before it erupted in 79 AD.

Writer and naturalist Pliny the Elder, at the command of a fleet of ships in the Gulf of Naples was interested in watching the volcano erupt. He advanced toward Pompey, where he met his death as a result of inhaling poisonous gases.

CONTENTS

MAP INDEX

HISTORICAL MAP

MAPS OF WINES REGIONS

PROLOGUE

The heritage of the wines of Chile is the universal story of wine. Wine is inextricably intertwined with the history of humanity, perhaps more than that of any other human expression. It has been present in man's story as far back as we have been able to reach. Wine was given a very special place in the first written testimony of man by the Greeks, by the Bible, and has maintained its importance throughout the ages in religious, ceremonial, cultural, and daily life. It has forever been the song of poets, from Ovid to Neruda.

Rodrigo Alvarado is particularly qualified to unite Chile and the modern world of wines to its extraordinary heritage. A gifted writer, a life-long observer of the wine world in which he has played important roles, and viticulturalist-enologist by training, he approaches the subject from a deeply humanistic point of view, which is his passion, yet with a thorough understanding of the technical aspects, an important element to comprehending the evolution of the process.

Wine is a product of people and place. From the first records available to us we learn that wines of certain places were more esteemed than others. This book takes us on a voyage through time and place, leading us to understand the positioning of New World Wines, specifically those of Chile, within the very rich spectrum of world wines. This is of special relevance in a world that moves ever faster toward globalization. Understanding wine's people and place is the basis for wine's historical diversity and interest. In this book, Alvarado makes a valuable contribution toward that end: he makes the wines of Chile very special.

Agustín Huneeus

INTRODUCTION

Historians should write history books and winemakers should make wine, so why write a good book about wine throughout the history of Chile and the rest of the world? This was the challenge that my editor put before me when I sketched out the first lines of this text. At first it seemed like a complex and daunting task, but with time and the support of historians and researchers, along with the generous collaboration of learned experts winemakers in Chile, Argentina, Uruguay, France, Spain, and the United States, we were able to bring this project to life.

This book invites the reader to embark upon a journey through time, from the origins of the vine 70,000,000 years ago, to the present day. In the ancient world, lands of the pharaohs, emperors, and gods, wine took its first steps and achieved a prestigious position. After the fall of the Roman Empire and during the Middle Ages, Christianity allowed for the resurrection of wine, establishing it as a fundamental part of European culture. In monasteries, feudal kingdoms, and peasant homes, knowledge of wine was slowly improving and later extended throughout the world in the 15th Century. Spanish and Portuguese Conquistadors brought the European vine to the New World, thereby initiating the history of wine in the Americas.

Meanwhile in Europe, the accumulation of knowledge and innovations resulted in a budding industrial development gave rise to the world's first fine wines, in certain regions of France. This process was brought to the Americas, particularly Chile, where aristocratic families entered into the wine business as an endorsement of their refinement and prestige.

As a result of the world wars in Europe, the heart of the modern wine world shifted to North America, where the technological boom gave rise to the use of stainless steel, better asepsis, temperature control, and other factors that led to significant advances in the wine industry. And thus both Europe and the New World began to produce excellent wines, arguably the best in all of history.

The objective of this book is to broaden the understanding of Chilean wines, beginning with a historical overview and global perspective, because this is the only way we can truly appreciate the tradition and essence of wine that stretch beyond matters of aroma, flavor, and color. This book is for every wine lover who has moved beyond the first stage of learning about wines and is ready to know more. Sit back, relax, and savor it with your intellect.

Rodrigo Alvarado

ORIGINS OF THE VINE
From Wild Creeper to Domestic Sativa

70,000,000 years ago, while wild cork trees, oaks, bay laurels, and ferns transformed the landscapes of the Earth, the wild vine crept and climbed among them. It was domesticated just 7,000 years ago and only then began its gradual change to the plant we know today.

V*itis*, the grapevine, emerged during the Tertiary Period, when the Earth was under the influence of glacial cold and the advancing ice modified the flora and fauna. In its wild state it climbed freely as a vine (liana), and with the rise of man and the later development of agriculture, it began to experience its long – though relatively short – evolution.

The first vines belonged to the Rhamnales family and appeared in a generalized form in Eurasia some 60 or 70 million years ago, thus initiating the long evolutionary process toward warmer climes in a time when the glaciers finally stopped advancing around the Mediterranean Sea and the southern part of North America. Vines belong to the genus *Vitis* and are subdivided into two sub-genera: *Euvitis*, which is present in Eurasia and North America, and Muscadina, which is exclusive to North America. In Eurasia, *Euvitis* contains 19 species, including *Vitis vinifera silvestris*, which later evolved into *Vitis vinifera sativa*, as a result of human intervention. This is the only species appropriate for winemaking.

In North America, the genus Euvitis is expressed in more than 30 species, many of which are used throughout the world for grafting *Vitis vinifera sativa*, as these American varieties are much more resistant to phylloxera. Only grapes of the labrusca variety are fermented to obtain wines characterized by their foxy aroma, which comes from an organic compound called methyl anthranilate, found exclusively in this species. In tastings, these smells and flavors are considered similar to raspberries. Another American sub-genus, Muscadina, consists of 3 species, of which berlanieri is the most important for grafting.

Human presence on Earth prompted a more pronounced development of the genus *Vitis*. The rise of sedentary communities stimulated advances in stonework and pottery as well as the adoption of new technologies that had bearing on crops. Draft animals, the plow, and new techniques such as irrigation and crop rotation helped the advancement of agriculture, improving the quality and quantity of the products and encouraging the occupation of new lands. Agriculture and the introduction of improved procedures led communities to favor settlements and larger populations. In this process, cereal crops became the mainstay of the ancient agricultural economy, an inheritance that was passed on to the cultures that arose later along the Euphrates, Tigris, and Nile Rivers, and still later to Greece and Rome.

The daily consumption of cereals was part of a diversified basic diet rich in fruits and vegetables; oils made of legumes, linseed, and olives; and beer and wine, which later became known as the Mediterranean diet. The step from collecting wild fruits to the discovery of agriculture was a revolutionary process that changed not only the way of life of the communities, but agricultural development throughout the world. Those movements affected the history of the vine, as its transformation from *Vitis vinifera silvestris* to *Vitis vinifera sativa* (from *satio*, meaning seed sowing or planted fields) marked the beginning of its cultural management and later planting of vineyards, where the creeping vine was trained against its nature to behave as a bush.

The development of this long-term process not only affected the plant, but those who cultivated it as well; it provided an indirect civilizing factor that encouraged early nomadic tribes to settle into sedentary groups. Unlike annual crops, the vine demanded year-round attention, obligating the communities to form villages that were transformed over time due to the need to create mechanisms to promote other crops, self-sufficiency, and later commerce. The origin of *Vitis vinifera* sativa has long been placed in Asia Minor, specifically in the area of Mount Ararat, east of Turkey, climbing into the Caucasus Mountains, between the Black and Caspian Seas. However, the discovery of new archaeological remains and DNA test results have demonstrated that the cultivation of *Vitis vinifera sativa* began simultaneously in different parts of Europe and Asia around 6000 BC, without affecting its survival in the *silvestris* form in many parts of Eurasia and elsewhere in the world.

Although it is still difficult to determine the precise moment when the wild creeper gave rise to the cultivated vine, we know it was not spontaneous but rather conditioned by human intervention. Through intuitive selection using criteria such as size, flavor, and resistance of the grapes, or the adaptability of the vines to the environment, etc., the evolutionary process rather quickly generated the *Vitis vinifera sativa* that we know today. This process of change was also related to an interest in understanding the origin of wine and improving the flavor and quality of the juice that appeared spontaneously from the harvested grapes, allowing us to assume that humans knew the flavor of wine before the vine had been domesticated. In effect, the first sedentary communities harvested

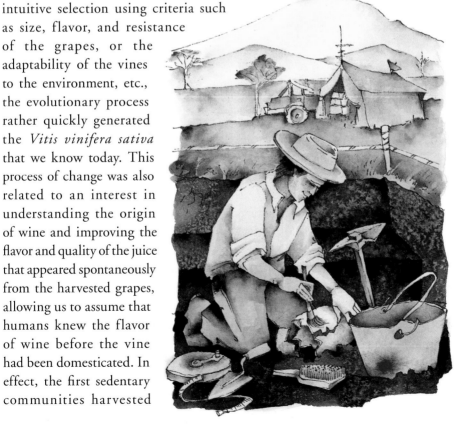

The origin of Vitis vinifera sativa was initially registered on Mount Ararat, although new archaeological evidence has shown that it was first cultivated in different parts of Europe and Asia around 6000 BC.

wild grapes (now *Vitis vinifera sativa*) that were consumed as fruit by the early inhabitants of Eurasia. It is likely that when these grapes were deposited into ancient containers, their juice spontaneously turned to wine. We cannot be certain of the moment in which humans first discovered fermented drinks, but it is believed that alcohol appeared with the first settlements. Some anthropologists maintain that fermented beverages made of dates, cereals, and small fruits such as blackberries, which were highly unstable, have been available in Europe for thousands of years. It is probable that a beer-like product was made by inducing fermentations from wild fruits, tubers, grasses (such as barley, oats, wheat, and rye) or other fresh ingredients that contain starch, which breaks down naturally and is capable of generating alcoholic fermentations. Making these drinks would have provided practice for making the first wines.

Widespread vine growing was established in Europe around 4000 BC, although there are indications that it actually began a couple thousand years earlier. With the increase in population of the Mediterranean and Asia Minor around 3000 BC, the first civilizations began to grow a variety of crops such as wheat, vines, and olives. In the Caucasus region, the juice of the fermented grape was given the name *voino*. This term, translated as 'intoxicating grape drink', was adopted and modified by ancient peoples, resulting in the Greek term *oinos* and the Roman *vinum*.

Grape growing and wine production were closely linked to the rise of agricultural technologies based on the initial domestication of *Vitis vinifera silvestris* and the later human intervention in the vitivinicultural process. This knowledge circulated throughout Europe and Asia Minor, covering long routes from the south of Europe and Caucasus to Mesopotamia, Egypt, Crete, Greece, and Italy, lands that slowly revealed the secrets of winemaking to the rest of Europe and later to the Americas.

Vitis emerged during the Tertiary Period. In its wild state, it climbed freely as a vine and with the rise of man and the later development of agriculture, it began to experience its evolution.

The close bonds between the histories of humankind and the vine show that the domestication of the vine could have been one of the first acts of agriculture. This in turn generated practices for obtaining not only grapes but wine, that magical drink that gave both life and meaning to the literature, mythology, fiestas, and trade of ancient cultures. The vine and its wine came to play a crucial role in the political, social, economic, and cultural relationships of the community, as is shown in Greek, Christian, and Hebrew texts, as well as the myths and legends that have been passed down to our times.

THE OLD WORLD
The First Steps Toward Wine

*In Ancient Egypt, vineyards were planted along the banks of the Nile.
Grapevines grew around small pools of water in domestic gardens and were
mixed with other plants, such as date palms, olives, poppies and other flowers.*

The origins of winemaking are located somewhere between myth and history, as told in the tales that introduce us to its magical powers and in clay tablets that record numbers and quantities sold. Art, literature, travel accounts, and scholars testify to the importance of this precious beverage and indicate that the foundations of modern vitiviniculture were laid during ancient times, largely due to the invention of new technologies, cultural exchanges, and the prestige of the wine itself.

Nevertheless, research into the beginnings of wine sparks a series of questions: How and when was wine discovered? When did humans first acquire the understanding necessary to produce it? Who was in charge of the winemaking process?

It is believed that the first wines were produced spontaneously when the juice of *Vitis vinifera sativa* grapes stored in clay jugs fermented, creating a juice with a higher alcoholic content than ever before known. This hypothesis is credible in that yeasts, the biochemical cause of fermentation, are almost always found on grape skins.

Other theories, however, claim that the process was produced along with the first cultivated vines, leading to the belief that *Vitis vinifera silvestris* did not contain enough sugar or the diversity of organic acids necessary to produce spontaneous fermentation and that therefore it was the human management of the vines and the transition to *vinifera sativa* that contributed to the process of generating wine. Regardless of the first advances, winemaking began to be widespread around 4000 BC, becoming incorporated into the different cultures as part of the daily diet, as a delicacy reserved only for the highest authorities, as an essential element of maritime trade, and as the beverage of the gods. Although it is still difficult to determine the first steps made toward winemaking and the route it must have taken subsequently, once it began to take hold, its historical path becomes much clearer.

The first wines were produced when juice from grapes stored in clay containers fermented spontaneously.

The Bible provides the first written references to wine. The book of Genesis allegorizes the settlement of the Earth by Noah and his three sons with the planting of the first vine after the Flood, establishing agriculture and vine growing as essential factors for cultural development and as a foundation for their future descents who would populate the Earth after the Arc came to rest on Mount Ararat. Despite the fact that there are various stories in the book of Genesis that make reference to the beverage, Noah's act of planting the first vineyard after the Flood, where the Echmiadzin Monastery is located today, portends the close relationship that wine would come to have in the different cultures as a symbolic beverage tied to the authorities and religion.

The chronologies traditionally used to determine the history of wine production in Europe not only follow biblical coordinates, but run parallel to the vitivinicultural production developed by early winemakers in the Near East, on the Iberian Peninsula, and along the Mediterranean coasts. However, it is interesting to study the history of wine beginning with the first civilizations of Asia Minor and the Middle East in that it contributes to the cultural, linguistic, religious, and commercial support that gave rise to wine in antiquity.

MESOPOTAMIA: THE WORLD'S FIRST WINE REGION

The fertile soils between the Euphrates and the Tigris were populated by sedentary agricultural groups around 6000 BC. Their first urban centers in the city-states of Ur and Eridu established the foundations of the ancient Sumerian culture, contributing to the commercial, written, religious, political, and agricultural development of the region. Cuneiform texts from the city of Kish dating back to at least 2500 BC inform us not only of the presence of vineyards in the region at that time, but of the wine trade that developed between the merchants of Lagash, close to the mouth of the Tigris, and the authorities of other Mesopotamian areas. This cultivation and trade was encouraged by the ruling class, which considered wine to be a symbol of fertility and reserved for a small elite group. Beer, on the other hand, was more abundant than wine and the alcoholic drink of the masses.

The establishment of the Acadians in the north of the region and their later conquest of the lower zones brought as a consequence the Sumerians' fall from power (2325 BC) and the expansion of the toward Mesopotamia's middle regions, particularly in the areas around the city of Babylonia. The trade boom that took place in those times due to the early contact with the region of Anatolia and Cappadocia increased the power of wine as an object of economic exchange and political prestige. It was not until Hammurabi rose to power in 1792 BC, however, that the wine trade in Mesopotamia became subject to legal restrictions. The regulations increased along with rules regarding hygiene-related food prohibitions for religious or commercial reasons. This was the first instance of official interference in the production and commercialization of wine, establishing the foundation of a system of control that has been maintained through to the present.

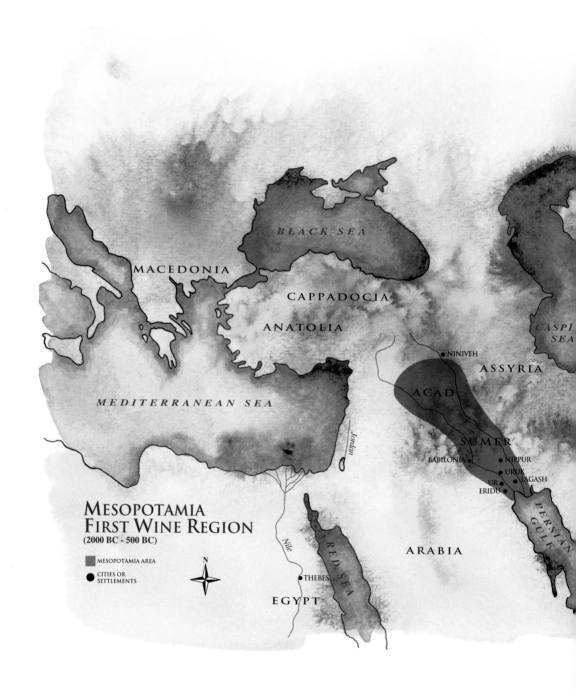

MESOPOTAMIA
FIRST WINE REGION
(2000 BC - 500 BC)

◼ MESOPOTAMIA AREA

● CITIES OR
SETTLEMENTS

N

BLACK SEA

MACEDONIA

CAPPADOCIA

ANATOLIA

CASPI SEA

● NINIVEH

ASSYRIA

ACAD

MEDITERRANEAN SEA

Jordan

SUMER

BABILONIA ●   ● NIPPUR

● URUK
UR ●   ● LAGASH
ERIDU ●

PERSIAN GULF

Nile

RED SEA

ARABIA

● THEBES

EGYPT

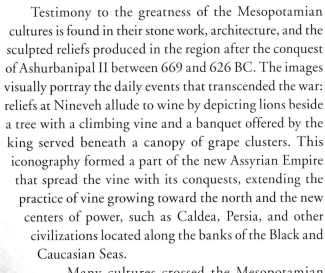

Testimony to the greatness of the Mesopotamian cultures is found in their stone work, architecture, and the sculpted reliefs produced in the region after the conquest of Ashurbanipal II between 669 and 626 BC. The images visually portray the daily events that transcended the war: reliefs at Nineveh allude to wine by depicting lions beside a tree with a climbing vine and a banquet offered by the king served beneath a canopy of grape clusters. This iconography formed a part of the new Assyrian Empire that spread the vine with its conquests, extending the practice of vine growing toward the north and the new centers of power, such as Caldea, Persia, and other civilizations located along the banks of the Black and Caucasian Seas.

Many cultures crossed the Mesopotamian Region over the course of 3,000 years, and it effectively spread its vine growing and wine making experience far beyond its geographical boundaries. While this occurred in the Near Eastern regions, the Egyptian civilization formed a unique entity in the Valley of the Nile that would be conserved for more than 3 millennia, due to the protection of its powerful natural barriers.

ERSIA

Indo

A Drink Fit for Pharaohs

More than 5,000 years ago, the Egyptians built a culture along the banks of the Nile River based on the figure of the Pharaoh, the worship of the sun god Ra, stonework, trade, and agriculture, a confluence that gave life to a rich civilization sustained for centuries and that guided the cultural development of the Mediterranean people. Beginning with the Old Kingdom (2647-2124 BC) the establishment of the administrative center in the northern part of the region produced a political stability expressed through the construction of enormous pyramid tombs. This required a massive work force, necessitating a change in agricultural methods, trade practices, and food and beverage production to feed the laborers.

Egyptian culture was rediscovered in the early 19th century, in large part through Jean-Francois Champollion's work in deciphering hieroglyphic writings, which in turn gave rise to modern Egyptology and a greater understanding of life along the ancient Nile. Oddly enough, one of the first symbols that Champollion was able to identify represented wine, which was called Arp.

Later research focused on understanding the religion, which was based on polytheistic worship and the belief in life after death. Their beliefs led to the development of the art of mummification as an essential rite for the journey to the next world. Bodies were thus treated, preserved, and laid to rest in elaborate tombs with sufficient space for their next life. Accordingly, the Egyptian funerary art that adorned the walls of pyramids and underground chambers included paintings and hieroglyphs that celebrated the most important aspects of life, politics, and religion. These images, along with the objects deposited in the tombs, provided the deceased with the comforts and atmosphere familiar to him or her in life. These illustrations have allowed us to understand the importance of wine in the Egyptian culture, as they depict scenes of the productive cycle as well as vineyards, harvest, vinification, and offerings to the gods according to their place in the hierarchy.

Agricultural development in the Egyptian region began with the arrival of the first sedentary communities around 5000 BC. However, it was not until 2000 BC that crop production intensified and expanded significantly, once methods were learned for organizing irrigation systems through a network of dikes and the introduction of the shaduf, a simple lever and counterweight mechanism for making the water rise. This allowed arable land to increase along with the population, giving rise to the legendary fertility of the lands around the Nile. They cultivated a variety of products, especially grains, that were valued both for volume and consumption.

One of the beverages most consumed by the Egyptians was "grain wine," better known as beer, which was made from red wheat that apparently came from the Palestine region. Although beer was consumed in Mesopotamia, it was the Egyptians who developed and produced it at a massive level by disseminating certain production methods used by women. They ground the wheat, kneaded most of the flour with water and let it ferment with yeast until it was ready for cooking. The part that was left unkneaded was then dampened and exposed to air and then later added to the mixture, which continued to ferment. The beer was sweetened with dates or honey and then stored in containers covered with baked clay and certified with a hieroglyphic inscription that specified its quality and authenticity.

The deep layer of lime found in the soils of the Nile was well-suited for grain production and helped feed the Egyptian people. Osiris, god of resurrection and fertility, was also considered to be the god of wine. Egyptian mythology shows him to be the first to teach the people to tend the vine and train it to climb a stake. He is also credited with the practice of making beer.

Although it is difficult to precisely determine when wine was first made in Egypt, literary and iconographic records portray the first vinifications as being very similar to those that took place in the late 18th century.

The lands around the Delta and the Fayyum oases were the most appropriate for planting vineyards as well as home gardens, which produced grapes on a smaller scale. Vines were cultivated in vineyards planted in an orderly fashion and in gardens next to the houses, where they grew around little pools of water along with other fruit trees and plants, such as olive trees, date palms,

After the grapes were gathered, they were deposited in stone containers, where they were crushed by foot. The resulting musts were left to ferment.

sycamores, poppies, and other fruits, flowers, and shrubs. Alcoholic beverages were not only made from grapes, but also from pomegranates, figs, dates, and palm sap, which was also used in the process of mummification. But wine was the drink of choice, and different types of red, white, and black wines were made. Some were also differentiated by names that designated their place of origin. Wines from the north, near Alexandria, were called Mareotic wines, while those from the city of Sebennytos were known as Sebennyte wines.

The Egyptians also drank imported wines, especially those from Syria, Palestine, and later from Greece. Images found in the Theban tomb of the astronomer Nakht, who lived and worked in the House of Amun from 1401 to 1353 BC, show the technology and processes used to turn grapes into wine. Grapes were gathered in wicker baskets, deposited in wooden or stone troughs, and tread by men supported by ropes attached to overhead beams to keep their balance. The resulting must was collected in a vat and left to ferment in clay containers that were sealed upon completion. Another system used in the Upper Nile Basin was explained by the Greek sage Strabo around 25 AC. His texts explain that once the treading process was completed, the skins were wrapped in a large woven cloth tied tightly between two posts and twisted to extract more juice, effectively creating the first wine press.

After the initial crush, the skins were wrapped in a woven cloth and twisted to extract more juice.

CHILEAN WINE. THE HERITAGE

The must was left to ferment in open containers to allow adequate ventilation. The container was later sealed, leaving a small hole so that the carbon dioxide formed during fermentation could escape. Once the fermentation was completed, the hole was covered, and the entire container was sealed with baked clay. As with beer, the ceramic containers carried the mark of the owner and established the wine's provenance through inscriptions that specified the quantity, origin, processing date, and point of sale. This provided information about the contents of the container and the life span of the product, which, in the case of Egyptian wines, was no more than one year. Once this period had passed, a mysterious phenomenon converted the wine into vinegar. The cause of this transformation was unknown until the 19th century, when chemist Louis Pasteur identified acetic bacteria, or acetobacter.

Except for the mechanization and technological advances that these methods have undergone, the vinification processes used by the ancient Egyptians were not very different from those used today. Curiously however, there are no clear records regarding the post-fermentation treatment of wine, such as how to separate it from its lees and obtain a clean and stable product. It is unlikely that these techniques were very advanced.

The quality of early wines did not reach the levels of excellence obtained later in Greece and Rome because neither Egypt nor Mesopotamia had the agricultural or climatic conditions necessary to produce high quality vines. However, the value of wine along the Nile was not measured solely from the perspective of quality. For the Egyptians, wine was an essential part of Mediterranean commerce, daily life, and religion as well.

Meals were an important daily ritual that took place three times per day in the upper classes. Peasants and workers ate large midday meal that included beer and bread. Many workers were paid with objects or other goods such as beer, fruit, vegetables, fish, and salt. Archaeological records of artisans and peasants homes show a variety of botanical remains, reflecting a rich and varied diet based on grapes, wheat, barley, lentils, dates, and olives.

Wine however played a central role in banquets and special events. As the preferred beverage of the authorities, it was a privilege reserved for the elite, and its consumption was limited to those who had vineyards on their lands. Wine was placed in the center of the tables during receptions and accompanied meals, games, and other recreational activities. Priests, men of great authority who ruled the temples and aided in the pharaoh's administration, were also involved in vine growing and winemaking, as is illustrated by the important vineyard Ka-em-Kemet at the House of Amun in Thebes.

Douro

Ebro

Tajo

ETRU

ALCÁCER DO SAL

LUCENTUM

PURGI

GADIR
MALACA
CARTEIA

THARROS
NORA

LIXOS

MOTIE
SOLU

RUSADIR
CARTENNA

TABRACA
CARTHAGE

ACHOLLA
USILLA

ILLYRIA

BLACK SEA

Danube

TRACIOS

GREECE

LIDIOS

MERIANDROS

LAPITHOS
BYBLOS
KURION
SIDON
TYRE

PHOENICIA

MEDITERRANEAN
SEA

CRETE

PHOENICIAN WINE MARKET
(900 BC - 300 BC)

EGYPT

LIBYA

GREEK TERRITORY

PHOENICIAN TERRITORY

CITIES OR
SETTLEMENTS

N

RED
SEA

Nile

NUBIA

The Egyptian contribution to the culture of wine is undeniable and is expressed in the social prestige of the beverage, its character as an exclusive offering, its registry as a liquid necessary in the afterlife, and its connection with Osiris, the god of festivals and fertility. The relationship established between wine and the divine was later passed on to the Greeks and the Romans in the figure of Dionysus and Bacchus, respectively.

Egyptian wine culture later spread and blended with those of Mesopotamia and Greece through trade, particularly by the seafaring Phoenicians, a culture of Semite origin that inhabited a narrow strip of the Syrian coast. From their beginnings, the Phoenicians were closely tied to trade, through which they exchanged Lebanese cedar for wheat and papyrus. As navigators, their mobility allowed them to interact with a number of other cultures, thereby becoming the first commercial and maritime power of the Mediterranean from 1200 to 750 BC. Their leadership resulted in the control of trade from Cypress to the Iberian Peninsula.

In addition to extending a communicational bond between the different groups, the Phoenicians also spread their most significant invention: the alphabet. Another of their lasting contributions is the expansion of the wine trade to markets from Asia Minor to the Mediterranean, where wine was exchanged for olives, sandalwood, perfumes, carpets, and other products. Around 600 BC, the establishment of the Phoenicians in settlements along the Mediterranean coasts aided in the importation of wine as well as the introduction of vitivinicultural technologies along the Iberian coast.

WINE EXPANDS WITH THE POLIS

Myths and legends say that the Greek god Dionysus brought the vine from the east. The stories show the contacts established by the people of the Middle East with the cultures of the Mediterranean coasts as a result of the diffusion of technologies and innovations through trade. The Aegean Sea and its various islands became the bridge between Africa, Asia Minor, and Continental Europe. Crete was particularly important for its fertile valleys and proximity to the region of the Phoenicians and the Egyptian coast.

At its peak in the year 2000 BC, the Isle of Crete owed its hegemonic position to commerce and the extension of its fleet. Its diminutive size made trade necessary and maritime might its primary source of wealth. The island embraced a palace culture that was especially characterized by the city of Knossos, the residence of the legendary King Minos and his son the Minotaur, whose death at the hand of Theseus symbolized the island's defeat to the continent. Its splendor lasted long enough to establish a sophisticated culture known for its peaceful customs, art, architecture, religion, respect for nature, and a love of sports.

Excavations of the Knossos and Malia Palaces led by Arthur Evans in the early 20th century shed light on the final days of these grand spaces that were used not only as homes and political centers, but as storage places for the island's grains, oil, and wine. The latter two products sustained an economy based on the cultivation of olives and vines and the commercialization of their derivatives. With large wineries and model warehouses equipped with containers and pipelines that greatly facilitated their manufacture, the palaces played a very important role in the production of wine and oil.

The decline of Crete began around 1600 BC with the arrival of Indo-European invaders who came from continental Greece and burned and destroyed the palaces and the villages that surrounded them. Fortunately, Crete's

Greek wine was associated with Dionysus, who was said to be the first to teach mortals to grow grapes and make wine.

heritage was preserved through the independent cities of Mycenae, Tiryns, and Troy, and was later incorporated into Greek culture.

These three cities were situated between history and epic tale and midway between the demise of culture of Crete and the beginning of the Greek civilization. Despite Troy's great fame, its image is shrouded in a veil of mystery. Homer's collected poems, dating to around the 8th century BC, explored part of this mystery and took shape in the Iliad and the Odyssey. He portrays the continuous change of the centers of power, the transfer of culture implied by the displacement of its inhabitants, and the fall of major cities. All of this allows us to understand the broad range of influences that provided the foundation of the Greek civilization, one of the most important sources of what would later become Western or Judeo-Christian civilization.

In the Iliad the confrontation between the Greeks and Trojans is a consequence of the kidnapping of the Greek Princess Helena by Paris, Prince of Troy, while the Odyssey tells the tale of Odysseus' journey home. These stories dramatize the commercial and cultural exchange that took place in the Mediterranean during the Mycenaean period, which directly affected wine by spreading the knowledge developed in Egypt and Mesopotamia through the west and vice versa.

Mycenae, which succeeded Crete, was located on the Argolis Peninsula, just north of Tiryns. Both cities were at their peak from 1600 to 1200 BC, when they began their decline with the invasion of the Dorians, whose presence marked the end of the Bronze Age, the onset of the Iron Age, and the beginning of a period of confusion that was subsequently brought to order by the rise of the Greek culture.

The final millennium BC was characterized by Greek hegemony, born of cultural exchange inherited from a number of cultures that inhabited the region, which lent a richness and cultural foundation to the new society.

The birth of this culture is closely related to its geography of small mountains and valleys that helped form an isolated and autonomous mentality that resulted in city-states, also known as *Polis*. These were located near hills that acted as a refuge (acropolis) and encompassed part of the surrounding land that allowed for the cultivation of certain products and self-sufficiency. Athens, Sparta, and Corinth, icons of the polis and examples of Greek culture, were located near the coast, favoring maritime contact, commerce, and cultural exchange.

Greek cities followed the already classic Mediterranean style of agriculture based on cereal, vines, and olives. Cereals were the most important in terms of mass production and popular utility, but there is no doubt that the production of olive oil was one of the most important agricultural activities. This did not prevent vineyards from having an honored place begun by the worship of Dionysus and the extent of commerce.

Pruning was performed early each year. This was a technique introduced by the Greeks to Italy and Provence. They then waited patiently for autumn to arrive and for the grapes to reach the necessary degree of ripeness. Harvest and the subsequent winemaking process began in September or October. The grapes were trod by foot in vats, and the resulting must was left to ferment in jugs that were usually buried in the ground. Part of the wine was distributed to slaves and laborers, and the rest was stored and treated until it became an exclusive product. Salt water, gypsum, and honey were used in an attempt to extend the conservation of the wines. Old wine was not considered good quality, and every effort was made to sell it quickly. For transport they used wineskins made of goatskins as sealed amphorae, waterproofing their interior with resin or oil, thereby attempting to avoid contaminating the wine and prolonging its life, an innovation unknown to the ancient Greeks.

Although Greek grape vine and wine production were originally intended to satisfy internal needs, the increase in demand created by the development of the city-state determined the growth of local production. New lands were cultivated with heavy reliance on slave labor. Vineyards complemented olive groves and wheat fields. Vine growing required greater care than other crops, as Hesiod and others described in texts intended to both educate and encourage the spread of agricultural practices.

Hesiod's 8th century BC writings, particularly *The Work and Days*, reveal a different world than that described in Homer's epic poems, works that discuss the daily life of a society confronting poverty and conscious of the possibility that the calendar, a drought, a fire, or war could deprive them of their means of survival. Hesiod's treatise provides guidelines for crop production, including grapes, and formulates an agricultural ideal based on the principle of autarchy: the dependence on native resources and the belief of the protection of the gods. Thus the foundations of Greek agriculture were laid, based on local production and on a religion that maintained a close contact between nature and the divine.

As Athens grew, Greek culture underwent a sustained and expansive development. The autarchic character of the city-state began to fade as Athens became the most powerful city of Greece. Due to its port Piraeus, Athens was able to use its military and political superiority for commercial ends. Its splendor was based on its great wealth, which encouraged democracy and the development of the arts, philosophy, and religious worship. Athens reached its height of glory under Pericles, who ruled during the *Golden Century of Greece* in the 5th century BC, when Greek culture grew and expanded throughout the Mediterranean.

The development of Greek wine culture was closely related to social wealth resulting from trade among the major polis. This meant transcending the local consumption phase in favor of trade, which in turn brought new techniques and better wines.

Greek vitivinicultural practices expanded along with their culture, radiating out beyond the Aegean Sea, the shores of the Black Sea, Sicily, the Mediterranean coasts, Egypt, and what is now southern France, where they introduced olives and vines to the ancient zone of Massalia, today Marseilles. The growing trade aided in the expansion of the crops, while new markets increased the volume of wine produced and the use of ceramics for storing and transporting wine and olive oil.

The Greeks were one of the first groups to define certain characteristics of wine and establish new enological practices. For example, the sweet wine called *pramnio*, which Homer mentions in the Iliad, was made of raisined grapes. Dioscorides, the renowned Greek physician who identified the grapevine and christened it *Oenophorus ampleos*, explained the process of making *pramnio* wine as practiced on the Island of Lesbos, where the grapes were dried by exposing them directly to the sun.

It was also common practice to add aromatic and clarifying substances, such as sea water, spices, honey, and resins. Presumably, sea water was used to moderate the unpleasant effect of high levels of both natural acidity and vinegarization (volatile acidity). Honey sweetened the wine and masked various defects, while raisins were considered a desirable complement. These ancient practices are used in Greece today to produce a wine called *retsina*. The peculiar flavor of these white wines has little in common with those we are used to drinking today, and there is little wonder why the only ones who continue to make and consume these wines are the Greeks.

Little is known about the stability of these wines, but it is possible that the Greeks employed elements that would be unacceptable by today's enological and sanitary standards. Nevertheless, the practice of sun-drying grapes to concentrate their fermented sugars made it possible to obtain wines with a very high alcohol content (over 16%), which in turn prevented the microbial action that decomposed the product, thereby achieving the desired enological stability.

The trade and shipping of wine was strictly regulated under Greek law. Wine could only be purchased in wide-necked containers if they were sealed. It could not be sold in small quantities taken from larger containers, which can be interpreted as a technique for avoiding the exposure of the remaining wine to air and contaminants. Furthermore, it was illegal to buy or sell wine on credit, and anyone caught acquiring wine from a future vintage was fined. Another restrictive norm prohibited Thassos Island ships from carrying foreign wines, which may well be the first protectionist act.

What did wine mean to the Greeks? What place did it hold in their culture?

The Greeks were great lovers of drama and theater, and their relationship with wine extended far beyond the technical aspects. Wine was also related to the worship of Dionysus, who was credited with teaching mortals how to grow grapes and make wine.

Greek writer Euripides mentions Dionysus in The Cyclops and presents wine as the best source of human happiness and as a god symbolizing the cyclical rebirth and seasonal renovation as a promise of the resurrection of the dead. Some believe that Dionysus was originally a minor deity and wonder why wine was associated with him instead of Demeter, the goddess of the fertility and a more important Olympian figure. One possible response is that wine may have been introduced to Greece from Egypt, and therefore its origin would have been attached to a minor deity. On the other hand, the earliest stories describe two ways of understanding wine: they warn of the effects of its abuse, and praise it for its sweetness and prestige.

With time the Greeks began to value the consumption of wine even more. In general, it was consumed in moderation and mixed with water. The first glass, it was said, was for health, the second for pleasure, and the third for sleep. Excesses were negatively associated with violence and madness.

In the symposium, or banquet, the Greeks gathered to drink and converse. Wines were believed to maintain debate and discussion.

Wine was used in rituals honoring Dionysus and as an offering to other deities as a symbol of blood. Another factor that gave it an important place in rituals was the fact that drinking wine in relatively moderate quantities produced a state of ecstasy that was interpreted as a means of approaching the gods. Other alcoholic beverages did not produce this effect, as no other fruit or ingredient reached the degree of concentration of sugars that grapes generated naturally. In temperate zones, wine easily reached 10% alcohol, which would be impossible with drinks made from dates or other fruits or beer, which barely reached 4%.

Dionysus also appears in myths as a liberating god related to the Near East who returned to Greece accompanied by a court of musicians, satyrs, and nymphs who inspired irrational and raucously chaotic festivals, such as those described by Euripides (480-406 BC) in his final tragedy, The Bacchae. These gatherings, where wine, women, music, and dance predominated, emerged as a type of protest against the rigid civic and political system that regulated life in the polis. Their dissident nature was later lost when authorities usurped the celebrations as a means of uniting the citizens and the state. The state-organized festivals and theatrical representations were limited to specific dates and territories, leading them to become false and fleeting spaces of freedom.

In The Bacchae, Euripides both individualizes and generalizes wine by attributing the following verses to it and Dionysus:

> "I come here from Lydia and Phrygia, from the golden region of Persia's sun-baked plains, from Bactria's walled towns, and the terrible country of Media. I have crossed all of Arabia, that land of promise; and the length and breadth of Asia Minor..."

It is easy to see how religion and the connection with Dionysus allowed wine to be incorporated into ceremonies and rituals and to finally occupy an essential place in Greek culture. But wine consumption was also tied to the metropolis and the commonplace; it not only became part of the Greek diet, but was used in the banquets and symposia as well. These gatherings are portrayed on 5th century Greek glasses, showing friends gathered at night to drink and converse. Wine was consumed in those events with the intention of maintaining debate and discussion. The president of the symposium determined the amount of water to be mixed with the wine, hoping that the participants would not become inebriated, although he rarely succeeded.

Wine was the preferred drink of the Greeks, and it formed part of the daily diet, which was usually composed of bread and lamb. It was also considered healthful and nourishing. It had psychotropic effects, granted social prestige, was an economically profitable agricultural product, and even approached divinity. It was from this perspective that Athenian historian Thucydides declared:

"The people of the Mediterranean began to emerge from barbarism when they learned to cultivate the olive and the vine."

In the 4th century BC, the century of Plato and Aristotle, prose began to flourish and Greek culture expanded through colonization and trade. Macedonia, the cradle of Phillip II and Alexander the Great, later became a wealthy region that rose to triumph over the Greeks and establish a new predominating influence.

In the hands of the Macedonians, Greek culture continued to expand into diverse parts of Europe and the Near East. Special attention was given to the area called Magna Graecia (Greater Greece), now Italy, where centuries earlier the Greeks had founded the colonies of Cumae near Naples around 750 BC, and Syracuse, in Sicily in 734 BC. These cities, along with others such as Sybaris and Crotona in southern Italy, or Naxos or Messina in Sicily, intermingled with local cultures, giving life to the new hegemony destined to reign over the Mediterranean: Rome. As a consequence, viticulture on the Italian peninsula was strengthened and Greek wines began their decline.

ROME AND ITS LEGACY TO WINE

Far from Greece, another region began to forge its own history. In the late 6th century BC, the Greeks began to populate the coast of the Italian peninsula, forming coastal city-states that origanally had little interaction with inland tribes.

Although the Phoenicians were the first to consistently transport and distribute wines throughout the Mediterranean, the Greeks are credited with having wrapped them in a cloak of culture and religion, which was later transferred to Rome in the figure of the god Bacchus, the heir of Dionysus.

When the Greeks colonized the southern coasts of Italy, they met with groups that already knew and grew wine grapes. Greek mythology states that Oenotrus, one of the sons of the god Lycaon and disciple of Aeneas, left the kingdom of Arcadia in the central region of Peloponnesus, en route to Italy, which they called Enotria, carrying with them the first vines and the knowledge necessary for winemaking. This myth supports the opinion of researchers who say that the name Italy comes from the ancient Greek name for the grapevine, *eit* or the Latin *vit*. Its root *al* derives from the Latin term *alo* to nourish, and together they form the terms *eital* and *vitalo*, meaning *land of the vines*.

In the beginning Greek cities enjoyed an economic prosperity that was largely due to the exploitation of agricultural resources. But the Greeks were not the only ones to colonize and initiate the urban boom in Italy. They were preceded by the Etruscans, who inhabited the peninsula's central zone and were involved in vine growing and winemaking. The union of the two cultures gave rise to

The Romans developed an excellent system of roadways, although they preferred river or maritime shipping methods for transporting wine in amphorae.

new technologies that would sustain agriculture and vitivinicultural development and accompany Rome for centuries.

Roman history begins when the Latin, Umbo, and Samnite tribes settled in the central valleys around 2000 BC. Iron was introduced around 1000-600 BC during which time the Etruscans arrived, followed by the Phoenicians and then the Greeks.

The Etruscans settled in the peninsula around 1000 BC, creating independent but confederated cities that were connected through culture and religion, political arrangement, and commercial ties. Around the 7th century BC they became the most powerful group on the peninsula, and their culture radiated from the north to Campania. Their love of wine has been documented from many brass pitchers depicted in funerary paintings that describe their banquets.

The city of Rome, founded by the Latins in the Lacio Valley, already associated with the Etruscans and other Italianate groups, slowly began to acquire greater presence and power. Rome did not move beyond its borders during the monarchic period (753-509 BC), and the Republic had to mature (509-27 BC) to witness the grandeur of the Roman Imperial period (31 BC-395 AD).

From Emperor Augustus to Trajan, Rome's power extended along with its borders. Its coffers were filled with the riches of trade and taxes, while its culture expanded throughout all of the newly-conquered lands.

In the beginning Rome extended its power the entire length of the Italian peninsula and then around the Mediterranean (or Mare Nostrum), which became, along with its other legendary routes, the primary space of commercial exchange. It was during the Imperial period that Roman power and presence reached its prime. The emperors, particularly Augustus, were concerned with beautifying the city of Rome, spreading the worship of Caesar, ensuring the conquest of the provinces, and developing literature and the arts.

Trade united an empire of more than 80,000,000 inhabitants that extended throughout Europe from the North Sea to the southern British Isles; from Asia Minor to the Black Sea; and from the Sahara Desert to northern Africa. Trade provided a means of communication, a way to learn of new crops and crafts, and an avenue for discovering previously unknown products. Commerce therefore stimulated agricultural development and the incipient industry. Italy began to sell its wines, oils, and amphorae in the Mediterranean, while Egypt contributed its papyrus and cereals, Gaul offered its meats and rich cheeses, and the Middle East surprised all with its exotic, rare and expensive products.

BRITANNIA

GERMANIA

ATLANTIC
OCEAN

Rhin

Danub

LUTECIA

GAUL

BURDIGALA
(BORDEAUX)

LYON

Douro

TOULOUSE

TOLOSA

RAVENA

Ebro

NARBO
MARTIOS
(NARBONNE)

MASSALIA
(MARSEILLES)

ITAL

Tajo

HISPANIA

TARRAGON

CORCICA

RO

SAGUNT

CERDEÑA

GADES

NEW CARTHAGE

MAURETANIA

CARTHAGE

EXTENSION OF THE ROMAN EMPIRE
(31 BC - 395 AD)

ROMAN TERRITORY

● CITIES OR
SETTLEMENTS

N

ILLYRIA

ADRIATIC

Oder

Danube

BLACK SEA

MACEDONIA

CONSTANTINOPLE

AEGEAN
SEA

APLES
POMPEY

TARENTUM

ATHENS

LYDIA

TARSO

SYRACUSE

MYCENE

SPARTA

CYPRUS

CRETE

MARE NOSTRUM

JERUSALEM

CIRENE

ALEXANDRIA

ARABIA

EGYPT

RED
SEA

Nile

THEBES

The most important trade route to the northern regions followed the Garonne River, passing through Toulouse toward the port of Bordeaux. The Bordeaux region became known as an early and major center for the distribution of wines from Aquitania and the Narbonne territory. This area included large extensions of swampy land, ill-suited for vine growing, that had to be drained before the first recorded vines could be planted there in 71 AD.

Vitiviniculture was of great importance to the Romans. Numerous Latin documents dating back to the times of the Republic in the 2nd century BC refer to vines and wines and their social and economic importance. These works gave rise to admirable technical treatises. The oldest of these texts, which unfortunately never reached the hands of modern historians, was written by Magon of Carthage (140 BC), whose treatise on agriculture included no fewer than 28 volumes, only 4 of which remain. After the destruction of Carthage in 146 BC, his texts were translated into Greek and Latin, providing a foundation for many later works.

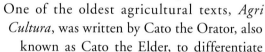

One of the oldest agricultural texts, *Agri Cultura*, was written by Cato the Orator, also known as Cato the Elder, to differentiate him from his grandson. His studies are known for their detailed analysis of the importance of vitiviniculture in the agrarian economy of the second-century BC Italian peninsula. He tells of the agricultural process based on the end of subsistence farming and local consumption and of the beginning of a stage where commercial activity would set the pace, essentially as a result of vine growing.

Cato's process took hold with the rise of the Empire, when vines were already cultivated for commercial purposes. This is demonstrated by large plantations worked by

First-century writer Lucius Junius Moderatus Columella perceived the influence of the land on the quality of the wine; his work is considered to be the first approach of terroir.

44

slaves, the disappearance of large numbers of family farms, and the transformation of independent peasants into vineyard workers or urban laborers. This was not a sign of the end of subsistence farming, but rather the emergence of a coexistence between the two systems of production. The increase in supply resulting from agricultural development motivated an increase in production and trade that went hand-in-hand with the development of the cities, as was also the case in Greece.

Cato's writings also offer insight into the annual viticultural cycle and details of vinification. He provides instructions for trellising, parcel size, the number of workers required, containers, presses, filters, and pruning tools. He also refers to vine nurseries, reproduction and transplantation methods, and stresses the importance and care of the press. He gives recipes for winemaking in which he mentions techniques similar to those of the Greeks, including drying grapes and adding saltwater to the mixture. His work is rigorous with respect to wine tasting, volume definitions, and wine storage, which he insists is the consumer's responsibility rather than the producer's.

Toward the end of the Republic (116 BC), M. Terentius Varro wrote in his *Rerum rusticarum* of the importance of different vine management systems, discussing five methods used in Italy: cuttings, canes, cords, reeds, and free method (head training).

We know that by the 1st century BC vines were planted in rows, a significant technical advance in that it allows greater sun exposure and protects the bunches from north winds. The Romans discovered at this time a number of winemaking and aging factors that would be used to determine the potential of different varieties of vines for generating wines of longer or shorter evolution times. Interestingly, Varro was the first to provide a written definition of the concept of economic loss.

Lucius Junius Moderatus Columella's 1st century work entitled *De re rustica* (65 AD) deserves special mention. Although the author was from Gades (now Cadiz), he lived most of his life in Lacio. His texts are considered to comprise the most important treatise on the agriculture of the classical world. His notable recommendations on choosing soils for planting vines and his examination of the influence of location on the quality of the crop and resulting wines could be considered a significant step toward the current French concept of *terroir*. Amazingly for his time, he proposed that those in charge of setting the date to begin harvesting first taste the grapes to evaluate their degree of ripeness, and adds that one should *"observe the color of the seeds."* He also offers recommendations on pre-harvest winery sanitation procedures and against the use of preservatives in the wines: *"as the best wine is that which delights us with natural quality."* It is interesting that Lucius Columella commented on the number of fortunes that have been lost in agricultural pursuits because:

> "…this activity is now very fashionable, and people jump into it without concern for the soil, vineyard location, or whether they even understand it sufficiently. They prune badly, exhaust their vineyards with excessive harvests that produce low-quality wines, and then they wonder what went wrong."

Pliny the Elder published an extensive list of the varieties and origins of the different wines consumed in the Roman Empire. His writings reveal his feelings about the changes in vine growing practices that took place during his lifetime, as well as his criticism of *"increasing productivity at the expense of quality."*

The writings of Pliny and Strabo lead us to believe that grapevines were widely grown throughout all of southern Europe and Asia Minor in the early Empire. When that was not the case, the Romans planted vines wherever soil and climate allowed it, such as in England and northern Africa, where production was essentially limited to local consumption. At that time, wines from the Italian peninsula were considered to be the best, especially those from the Lacio area. Widely exported wines from Baetica and Tarraconense in Hispania were also considered excellent.

Vine growing for winemaking tended to develop along the Mediterranean coast or navigable rivers because although the Roman roads were excellent, it was difficult and costly to transport wine in clay amphorae by land. This made river or maritime shipping preferable to overland transport, even when it meant crossing the entire Mediterranean rather than traveling a mere 100 kilometers by land.

Wine was consumed by women, men, peasants, and foreigners of every social group that could make or buy it. Roman poets describe the extent of its demand. The *convivium*, which means invitation in Latin, was a common event that allowed the presence of women. Wine was the proper vehicle for this gathering of pleasure and love, although it did not have the wild connotation of Bacchanalian affairs. A *convivium* was similar to the Greek *symposium* in that it was a social activity based on food and drink. As in other cultures, it symbolized social promotion or belonging to a group of power and influenced aspects of luxury, clothing, household furnishings, and tableware.

The use of wine for medicinal purposes was passed down from the Greeks. Particularly important were the recommendations of Hippocrates of Chios (460-377 BC), who prescribed it as a disinfectant for wounds, fever reducer, purgative,

The Romans transported wine in dolias, large containers attached to the interiors of ships. Salt water was added to preserve the wines.

and diuretic. Claudinus Galenus, better known as Galen, the second-century Greco-Roman physician, based his work on the teaching of Hippocrates. The same line was later used by physicians in the Middle Ages.

One of the most important innovations in the process of winemaking was the adoption of wooden barrels, which were first used by the Gauls for beer. Julius Caesar discovered them during the conquest of Gaul (1st century BC), which also resulted in the introduction of grape vines into the Bordeaux region. Wine production in Gaul gave rise to the use of new varieties better suited to the climate, resulting in a new concept of quality, which until that time had been based on sweetness.

Barrels were also gradually substituted for amphorae as the preferred method of transporting wine. The 19th century German archaeologist Heinrich Dressel's discovery of amphorae or clay vessels for wine provides a nearly exact view of the extent of agricultural trade achieved by the Romans. In his 1899 book *Corpus Inscriptionum Latinarum*, Dressel classified more than 45 types of amphorae, and by studying the symbols used on them, he was able to determine the fluvial and maritime routes used by the Romans as well as the quantities of wine transported throughout the Empire. These ancient containers, still used today to store olive oil, fruit, and even fish, were first made in the mid-second century BC, and were inspired by designs inherited from the Greeks. The pointed base was inserted into

During the festivals in honor of Bacchus, semi-nude priestesses were crowned with clusters of grapes, vines, and tendrils and pursued by the priests of Bacchus. These wild festivals gave rise to imaginable excesses.

CHILEAN WINE. THE HERITAGE

the sand to provide balance and allow the contents to mature. The amphorae were improved over time to make them larger and lighter. The most common amphora weighed 25 kg and held 0.88 liters per kilo.

When the Romans arrived in Hispania, the local people were already familiar with basic vinification techniques. Once they reached the borders of the Ebro River however, they began to teach the new members of the Empire their procedures for obtaining wine by pressing grapes in stone troughs and leaving the musts to ferment naturally.

The Romans differed from the Greeks in that they began to seal the wine with a stopper made from a piece of resin-covered bark from the cork tree. This early use of cork partially replaced the Greek clay seal and the practice of spreading oil, salt, honey, or tar over the surface of the wine to preserve it.

One innovation for maritime transportation was the use of the large containers called dollium or dolias, which were incorporated into the ships. These were apparently experimental in nature as they did not last long and were abandoned around the first century BC. Dolias were the precursors to the tanks used today for storing large volumes of wine. Their failure as shipping containers can be explained by the fact that as there were neither pumps nor hoses in those days; the liquid had to be transferred manually using small buckets, at high human and economic expense. Dolias continued to be used as stationary containers until well into the Middle Ages, when they were gradually replaced by wooden barrels.

The commercial significance of wine during the Empire, as well as the relationships established with other goods such as amphorae and skins, influenced certain regulations that began to circulate during the Roman Empire. At the end of the first Christian century, Emperor Domitian enacted legal restrictions for the expansion of vine growing with the aim of ending the overproduction of grapes, a phenomenon that occurred around the year 79 AD. The excess of vineyards and a shortage of grains provoked a crisis that was resolved by a prohibition against planting new vines.

Toward the 3rd century AD prices increased due to a rise in inflation that led Emperor Diocletian to create laws to set the price of wine and stop speculation. It is not surprising that these regulations not only failed to achieve their objective, but rather intensified the phenomenon, a trend that would be repeated frequently over the ages and into modern times.

For the Romans, wine was not only important in the commercial sense, but was also strongly tied to religion, as it was in Greece. Dionysus crossed over into Roman mythology and became Bacchus, derived from *Bakkos* in the Lydian language. This deity, considered to be the son of Jupiter, was identified with vegetation, and was represented on drinking vessels with a horn full of drink and grape clusters. He was also considered to be the god of wine, fertility, death, tragedy, and the defender of women.

Bacchus is also associated with the orgiastic cults of the bacchantes or maenads: "mythical women" who wandered through the forests in a state of ecstasy produced by their proximity to Bacchus. They practiced their rites in the *bacchanals*. These religious festivals passed down from the Greeks to the Romans became increasingly wild over time, and the ensuing Bacchic furor (drunkenness and lust) gave rise to every imaginable excess. The bacchantes, or priestesses, played a central role in these festivals: semi-nude, with their long hair flowing loose and carrying flowers or lighted torches in their hands, they danced and played cymbals, tambourines, or flutes to the point of exhaustion. They were always crowned with bunches of grapes, vines, and tendrils. Other participants included Bacchus' priests, also called bacchantes, satyrs, faunus, and silenos.

Around 186 BC, the Roman Senate prohibited bacchanalian celebrations, which were by then considered to be contrary to the Roman spirit. The mystery of Bacchus remained, and he continued to be worshipped secretly until Julius Caesar reversed the ruling and allowed the celebrations once again.

Great fortunes were amassed in the wine business, as was the case of Roman millionaire Marcus Porcius, who financed the amphitheater of Pompey with income earned from wine.

CHILEAN WINE. THE HERITAGE

The legendary city of Pompey was a center of pleasure, wine, and trade. Located at the base of Mt. Vesuvius, in the gulf where Naples now sits, Pompey was completely destroyed when the volcano erupted in 79 AD and buried the city under rock and ash for more than fifteen centuries. Later excavations that began in 1748 have provided great insight into the daily life of the Romans and their relationship with wine. Paintings, mosaics, houses, and patios remain intact throughout the city and reveal the significance of the beverage to the Romans in both dietary and religious aspects. Pliny the Elder, author of the afore-mentioned agricultural treatise, was among those who died in Pompey. As commander of a fleet of ships west of Naples, he safely witnessed the eruption of Mt. Vesuvius from a distance. But as a naturalist, he was interested in observing the phenomenon more closely and approached Pompey, only to die as a result of toxic gas.

Pompey, or the *City of Bacchus*, was a luxurious urban center with a heterogeneous mass of men and women who strolled the streets seeking entertainment and recreation. Famous for its numerous brothels, it welcomed wealthy merchants who decorated their homes with murals that alluded to love and wine. Great fortunes were made in producing and selling wine, as was the case of Roman millionaire and wine merchant Marcus Portius, who funded the expenses of the Pompeian amphitheater.

For centuries Rome provided unity and tranquility to the lands of the Mediterranean, encouraging trade, cultural exchange, and of course wine production. Its legacy extended into the Middle Ages, the historical period that reinforced the union of wine and religion, its presence in the upper social spheres, and its commercial importance.

Toward the 5th century, a political crisis began that brought periods of military anarchy. The construction of the city of Constantinople and Emperor Constantine the Great's conversion to Christianity laid the groundwork for the division of the Roman Empire. These civil wars hindered trade and the circulation of the population, generating internal disorder that weakened Rome's ability to protect its borders, thereby allowing the barbarians to enter. The first invaders' initial advances were slow and peaceful, although they presaged a future where the massive raids of Germanic, Frank, and Goth tribes would provide the final blow to an empire in crisis and decadence. The end of the Roman Empire in the west in 476 AD provoked the Roman retreat to the eastern territories with a seat in Constantinople.

THE MIDDLE AGES
The Resurrection of the Vine

The powerful symbolic significance of wine in Christianity contributed to its spread and survival during Medieval times. The art of wine improved and grew in the monasteries and feudal estates until it became an essential part of European culture.

The barbarian invasions pillaged and plundered the Western Roman Empire for two hundred years, producing instability and paralyzing commercial, industrial, and cultural development. Europe would later rise again in a new order, and Germanic, Frank, and Roman cultures blended to form the foundation of future medieval societies that slowly converged into new political centers that would later shape the European kingdoms.

The Church and the Monasteries

In the 5th century AD, after the fall of the Roman Empire in the west, wine and vitiviniculture survived, in large part with the aid of Christianity. Church doctrine endowed it with a powerful symbolic and religious content, reinforcing the significance passed down through centuries of Greek and Roman tradition. We cannot, however, credit Christianity exclusively with the survival of wine, as its prestige was inherited through historic tradition.

Christianity's beginnings in Rome's eastern territories during the early centuries of the Empire had its influence on wine and its productive process. Christian rites celebrated the Eucharist, in remembrance of Jesus' Last Supper with his disciples, in which the consecrated bread and wine took on vital importance as the body and blood of Christ.

It can be deduced that the symbolism of the vine in representation of Christ conserves the Dionysian-Bacchic imagery, presenting continuity in the relationship that wine established with the divinities of the Roman and Greek past. From there the necessity of expressions such as that of St John, *"Christ is the true vine,"* which attempts to differentiate the iconography of Jesus from the pagan images related to the vine. This use of symbolism has roots in the Old Testament, in which the people of Israel were also represented as the true vine.

From the beginning of Christianity, the use of wine in celebrations and gatherings was prudent. For example, St. Paul cautioned Timothy,

> *"Don't drink pure water, mix it with wine for your stomach and your frequent illnesses." (1 Timothy 5:23).*

Likewise, Christ's first miracle occurred when he turned water into wine at the wedding at Cana. But both examples allow other interpretations. Some see the remaining influence of Dionysus, who turned water into wine in Greek mythology, while others see it as a sanitary measure; there is no doubt that the alcohol in the wine would make the water safer and healthier.

Despite their tolerance for new religions, Roman authorities persecuted the early Christians because they considered their beliefs contrary to the official religion of the Empire, which was centered on the figure of the Emperor. Christianity's monotheistic nature rejected the Roman gods and the worship of the Emperor in public rituals.

Roman condemnation explains Christianity's 200-year silence and secretiveness. Emperor Constantine the Great ended the persecution in 313 AD by promoting religious tolerance in the Edict of Milan, thus paving the way for Christianity's route toward becoming the primary religion, with wine positioned in its rituals well above other ancient traditions. Decades later, Spanish-born Roman Emperor Theodosius set in motion the definitive triumph of Christianity in Rome by declaring it the official religion of the Empire in 395.

The arrival of the Visigoths and Germanic tribes to the center of power of the ancient Roman Empire generated a period of instability that brought the wine trade to a halt. The newcomers to the Mediterranean during the 5th and 6th centuries did not destroy the vineyards but continued to grow vines, although on a small scale at first. The Barber, Swabian, Vandal, and Burgundian kingdoms in Gaul and Hispania in the early 5th century had worked the vineyards to produce wine for local consumption.

After the fall of the Roman Empire, the region suffered a severe economic crisis. This, combined with the appearance of epidemic illnesses such as smallpox and cholera and the subsequent significant decrease in population, was more devastating than the barbarian invasions. Within this dismal context, Christian religious communities, already institutionalized in a Church, concentrated the cultural monopoly of the knowledge of classic culture.

Christianity spread throughout Europe in the form of isolated communities that later culminated in the creation of monasteries that would play an essential role in the development of wine. They encouraged education, preserved the original manuscripts of the Roman treatises, and kept the knowledge and techniques of agricultural and industrial production alive and current.

Christian monks, particularly the Cluniacs and the Cistercians, lived a life of reclusion that paradoxically influenced the development of vitiviniculture and

Wine has always played a highly symbolic role in Christianity. During the Last Supper of Jesus and his disciples, the bread and wine were consecrated as the body and blood of Christ.

economic progress in western Europe. They turned their convents into major agricultural centers by establishing an economy of self-sufficiency that later expanded into a system of trade with neighboring towns and villages. The monasteries' need for wine for daily consumption and for celebrating the Eucharist obligated them to have their own vineyards and master the technology and knowledge required for wine production.

Due to its resistance and adaptability, vine growing continued to increase with the help of priests and monks who took the process to the most distant corners of Europe. The knowledge concentrated in the monasteries affected the productive development of wine in the sense that the priests sought to improve its flavor and understand its medicinal qualities. Thus St. Benedict indicated the need to drink a quarter liter of wine per day, either plain or with thyme, to combat digestive problems, anemia, and dysentery.

Despite the historical importance of wine in Christian liturgies and rituals, there were no regulations for its consumption in the beginning. Early Christians celebrated the Eucharist with blessed wine, a practice that was maintained until 1215, when the Fourth Council of Letran prohibited lay members of the Church from taking communion with wine, limiting its use to the priest who officiated the mass. Later reformists of the 14th and 15th centuries rejected the prohibition, and the generalized use of holy wine was reinstated in many places until the 1414 Council of Constance once again restricted its use to the officiating priest.

The importance of the monasteries and the church is undeniably very significant in the preservation and development of wine. This does not imply, however, the absence of viticulturists outside the religious sphere. In fact, their presence and work was essential to protect the crops from barbarian invasions and the end of the imperial order. Therefore, despite the importance given to the action of the clergy in the production of wine between the 5th and 10th centuries, we must recognize the role played by peasants and small farmers who maintained production for local consumption in small towns and villages.

Along with the development of monastic communities, the political organization that began to take shape around the 8th century helped the rise of commercial trade networks that influenced agricultural development. The installation of a Frank kingdom led by Clodoveo (482-511) was one of the first indications of the recovery of political order. His successors, the Merovingios kings, delegated their governmental responsibilities to their palace officials, which gave rise to the 8th century Carolingia dynasty, considered to be the driving force behind another rebirth of vitiviniculture.

Meanwhile, the political center shifted northward, primarily under the authority of Charlemagne (768-819). His conquests included part of today's France, Belgium, Netherlands, and Germany. The northerly climes certainly must have made vine growing difficult, and therefore wine was extremely expensive and only available to the rich. The presence of the vine has also been confirmed beyond the Rhine, as German monasteries were involved in vine growing in Eastern Europe.

THE INFLUENCE OF ISLAM

During the 7th and 8th centuries, Europe confronted Islam, the religion that dictated new practices and bestowed new symbolism upon wine and the vine. Islam arose in Arabia around the 6th century with the birth of the profit Mohammed and expanded with unprecedented speed, encompassing Syria, Palestine, Jordan, Persia, Alexandria, Carthage, Hispania, Sicily, and other territories. Islamic progress was surprising; after crossing the Strait of Gibraltar and conquering the Visigoth kingdom in 711 AD, it easily established itself in the Iberian Peninsula for more than 700 years.

Islamic Spain reached great prosperity under Moorish rule. Extensive canal systems were built, and the introduction of new products: saffron, rice, and fruits such as peaches, apricots, and oranges, stimulated agricultural development in the region. The Moors established new trade networks that initiated a period of economic and commercial resurgence based on relationships with the east. Their ships and caravans traveled across Europe, contributing to Mediterranean trade with Alexandria, Damascus, and other areas. Despite the new agricultural context introduced by the Arabs, their arrival also brought the Koran's prohibition of alcohol, which had major consequences for vine-growing, and obviously for winemaking as well. The Koran instructs its followers:

> "They will ask you about wine and games of chance. There is great sin in both, and advantage as well to men; but their sin is greater than their advantage." (Sura 2: 215).

> "O believers! Surely wine, games of chance, statues, and the divining arrows are an abomination invented by Satan! Avoid them, and you will be happy." (Sura 5: 92).

The arrival of the Muslims on the peninsula prompted a split between the Arabian and the Christian Middle Ages. Interestingly, despite cultural differences and the Islamic prohibition against alcohol consumption, a portion of the grapes grown for fresh consumption were separated for small-scale vinification. Regardless of the prohibitions, the Muslims of Al-Andalus consumed enough wine to stimulate active trade among the different cities of the peninsula. Ironically, the Arabic word for wine, pronounced *Khamn*, came to refer to all alcoholic drinks and has been presented as a factor of happiness in the Moslem paradise.

> *"Here is a picture of the Paradise promised to those who fear God! There are rivers of water, which corrupt not; rivers of milk whose taste changeth not; and rivers of wine, delicious to those who drink it; and rivers of clarified honey, and every type of fruit, and pardon for their sins."*
> *(Sura 47: 16-17).*

Wine comes to embody the tension between that which is forbidden and that which is desired, between pleasure and renunciation; wine therefore becomes the icon of the excesses that must be avoided to enter Heaven. This duality allows us to understand the historic variability in enforcing the Koran's prohibition on wine consumption, which varied substantially among the different Islamic groups, even in the early years of its observance. The existence of different viewpoints produced moments of less control and others of greater fundamentalism that exacerbated respect for Koranic law and prompted further destruction of the vineyards.

The theoretical proscription on vine growing for wine production had some interesting technical effects, primarily in the selection processes that sought after better production of grapes for fresh consumption. The Muslims wanted to increase crop size, produce sweeter grapes, and eliminate seeds, the precursor to the first seedless grapes. Furthermore, the variety Sultana (known as Thompson seedless in the US, the largest producer and consumer), the most popular variety of table grapes today, originated under the norms inspired by the inhabitants of the Islamic peninsula. In these circumstances its name, Sultanan (or Sultanina), seems to phonetically evoke the word *sultan*, the generic name of a Moslem leader. Technically speaking, seedless grapes were simply the small grapes that produced little raisins, called sultaninas or sultanas. Physiologically, it is impossible to conceive of the existence of large grapes without seeds because they provide gibereline, a hormone essential for the development of the grape berry. In modern viticulture this hormone is applied artificially to stimulate the development of the berry.

The arrival of Muslims on the Iberian Peninsula sparked a cultural transformation expressed in many facets of Hispanic society. Language, art, social rituals, food, drink, and especially the process of grape production, all experienced innovations. Vitiviniculture was not eliminated, and wine production continued, as the restrictions remained primarily on the level of apparent orthodoxy. Constant warnings against alcohol consumption aimed at ascending sovereigns and the population at large, along with numerous strategies employed to elude controls, such as the use of grape syrup to conceal the wine, reveal that wine was consumed at every level of society. The prohibition did, however, succeed in halting large-scale production, such as the formation of international trade that would have encouraged improvements in the vitivinicultural processes of the Iberian Peninsula.

In the Spain of the Reconquest, viticulture spread with the advance of Christianity. It was sustained in the different kingdoms and monastic orders, where it was developed in tandem with the reunification and enlargement of the peninsula.

"Satan wants to incite hatred and opposition among you with wine and gambling and to distance you from God and prayer. Will you not abstain from this?" (Sura 5:93)

Wine Production in Feudal Times

In the 9th and 10th centuries, new invaders arrived in western Europe. Normans, Saracens, Slavs, and Hungarians advanced across the territories destroying the structure of their political order and dividing the lands governed by the descendents of Charlemagne. The resulting insecurity and disorder generated new relationships of power based on protection and service, which took shape in the feudal system. Agriculture was established as the primary source of wealth and gave rise to a strongly agricultural society. Conquests and anarchy limited the cities and encouraged ruralism, small property, countrysides abundant in vineyards, animals, and fields of grains and vegetables that formed the primary source of nourishment. Autarchy and local consumption increased as economies became confined and commercial trade decreased.

Large landowners began to assume a greater political power as their control over the land took on unprecedented importance. Peasants sought the landowner's protection in exchange for work and service. In this sense the authority of the king was replaced by that of the feudal lord, who monopolized agricultural production along with military and political power in his region.

The feudal lords, who were largely noblemen, surrounded their castles with vineyards that produced wines for house consumption. The search for quality to satisfy their own demands and to impress visitors was certainly an incentive for improving the characteristics of the product, despite the fact that the lack of commercial markets slowed the development of vitivinicultural production. This paralysis explains to some degree why wine consumption during those years was concentrated in exclusive groups: the clergy and those belonging to the highest social classes.

Townspeople and peasants drank fermented fruit juices and beer, and occasionally wine of rather dubious quality. It is worth noting that the consumption of beer was very common, as not only was it easier to produce than wine, but its lower alcohol content limited drunkenness and its consequences.

The feudal lords, who were largely noblemen, surrounded their castles with vineyards that produced wines for house consumption.

Agricultural advancements such as the water mill and improved in farming tools, along with the expansion of agricultural land at the expense of the forests, resulted in increased areas planted to vine. The expansion of the crop had a bearing on those who worked the land and the community that profited from wine. The process intensified during the harvest, and women were responsible for picking the grapes. Fermentation was considered not only a means of obtaining a delicious product, but also part of the technology of food conservation for the winter months and periods of famine and drought. In this sense, the process sought to conserve

the essence of the drink and maintain its caloric contribution; in the case of beer this constituted a significant percentage of the daily calorie intake.

Despite this progress, however, a technical overview of the year 1000 indicates that the vitiviniculture of the day had still not returned to the levels reached during the Roman Empire. There are no known texts of the magnitude of Columella's work, but we do know that many monasteries conducted their own research and that in those years they had already begun the process of defining some vine varieties.

The concept of ageing wine as it had been practiced by the Romans was lost during the Middle Ages. Hermetic clay containers such as the amphorae and dolias were slowly replaced with rudimentary wooden vessels, a practice passed down from the Gauls. Their larger storage capacity and the cylindrical shape allowed them to be rolled like a wheel, an advantage that took priority over the quality of the product. However, the contact of the wine with the wood constituted a first step toward discovering the positive complement between the two elements, a relationship that would eventually become essential for high-quality winemaking. It is important to mention France's good fortune in having oak trees that are especially appropriate for these ends; only California and Bosnia can say the same.

The extension of the vineyards increased between the year 500 AD and the first millennium, largely due to improvements in overland transportation and the local activities of noblemen, the clergy, and monks. Although it is difficult to calculate vineyard density and dispersion with any precision, it has been shown that by the year 1000, the vine had spread beyond the territory of the Roman Empire, extending into what is now Alsace under the Carolingians, and north into what is now Hungary. Aided by the stability of the Eastern Roman Empire, wine continued to flourish in the Middle East along the Mediterranean coasts. It did falter, however, in the early 7th century with the imposition of Islamic religious principles at the hands of the Moors, resulting in a major reduction in vineyards and wine consumption.

With respect to the Far East, vine growing extended into northeastern India and along the Silk Route, although wine never became a popular beverage in this area. Nor did it succeed in China, where preference was given to a low alcohol rice beverage, known as white wine or green wine and perhaps similar to the sake consumed today in Japan.

In the southern sectors, vitiviniculture withstood the presence of the barbarians without major problems, although throughout the Iberian Peninsula, the Islamic invasion restricted the cultivation of the vine in the south, limiting it, at least in the formal sense, to the northern provinces.

MEDIEVAL MERCHANTS AND MARKETS

The process of reversing the setbacks experienced during the early Middle Ages began with the introduction of increasingly accelerated changes that started in the 11th century. These changes gave shape to new advances in different areas of creativity and human work, thereby initiating a period of adventure, expansion, and revolution.

While Romanic architecture brought the vitiviniculture of medieval monasteries to light, the keenness of the Gothic style portrayed a period of renaissance that began to take shape during the first centuries of the new millennium. Literary works such as Dante's Divine Comedy, new philosophical expressions, discoveries in the area of navigation, and a series of advances in human thought emerged as an expressive gesture of the changes experienced in Europe. The rise of new urban structures, the growth of towns and villages, and the presence of major trade cities stimulated the development of regional sentiments.

The wine trade expanded toward parts of the world that had never before grown vines or made wine. After the cultural fusion with the peoples of the north, it moved in that direction as well. It was necessary to modify the sweetness of wines from these colder regions as a primary criterion of quality, generating new directions in enology.

During this time, new texts appeared that describe the vitivinicultural activity of the day. The first of the major differences between traditional Mediterranean winemaking and that of the north was that the former, based on the exploitation of olives and grain crops, was developed for family subsistence, while the latter was oriented toward export markets. This commercial trade was primarily based on fleets that sailed from the Mediterranean coast of France to England, incorporating the markets and economies of major medieval ports such as London, Bordeaux, and Bruges along the way.

One of the most important cities of the time was Bordeaux, known for both commerce and vitivinicultural production, which later transformed it into the world's fine-wine capital. Bordeaux wines were in demand by the English, who purchased more than half of its exports, reaching close to 80,000 tons per year. The rest of the production was exported to other regions of France, Flanders, and northern Germany. Toward the mid-15th century, English political supremacy over the region of Aquitaine ended, drastically reducing exports and negatively affecting the city's prosperity. The Dutch, who had been small buyers of Bordeaux wines, became the substitute for the English market, trading the wine world-wide. The Dutch preference for white wines is also attributed with having motivated the production of white wines in Bordeaux. The English and the French, on the other hand, preferred lightly colored red wines called *clarets*. At that time full-bodied red wines were little appreciated and were primarily for export, as they had the structure necessary to resist long journeys.

It has been shown that the vast majority of feudal castles and monasteries were equipped with presses and other basic vinification systems. These apparatuses were rented out to peasants and small farmers in exchange for part of the wine obtained. The custom became so rooted in medieval society that it later gave rise to wine cooperatives that have remained active throughout the centuries to our times.

The knowledge that was passed down from the Middle Ages is partially due to the preservation of sources that recount the agricultural system and vitivinicultural practices of the day.

English merchants bought Bordeaux wines to sell in London. In the 15th century, the Dutch monopolized the Bordeaux wine trade for distribution throughout the world.

CHILEAN WINE. THE HERITAGE

Among the most complete texts known from the period are those of Arnaldo de Vilanoba, a Valencian Jew (1245-1312) who wrote *De Vinis and Regimen Sanitatis*. This work recommends drinking wine to prevent heart attacks and improve eyesight, as one of its principle effects was to lighten the blood. Vilanoba was also a renowned physicist, and in his writings he referred to adapting an Arab innovation that he used to obtain a type of brandy through the process of distillation. Another highly regarded author of the day was Petrus de Crescentis, who studied viticultural procedures in the Roman Empire and wrote *Libier Commondorum Ruralium* in 1309.

Other less important works depict a concern for diversity in their references to specific grape varieties that experts have been able to relate genetically to current varieties, such as Pinot Noir in Burgundy in the 16th century.

Much of the knowledge and technique employed can be observed in the iconography of the day. For example, the engravings that appear in *Le Très Riches Heures* du Duc de Berry, published in 1413, present agricultural tasks and practices conducted throughout the year.

The progressive pace of regional peace and political stability motivated the rebirth of urban life and created the environment necessary for the resurgence of commercial exchange. During this period, cities formed during the Roman Empire, such as Paris, Brussels, London, Cologne, Nuremberg, and Barcelona, grew considerably. This stimulated an increase in the European population, estimated at 60,000,000 in the year 1400.

As a consequence of urban renovation, merchants became more important by increasing their acquisitive power and the control of the market. This bourgeois social group strengthened the image of wine as a symbol of status, economic power, and social position. Meanwhile, wine was slowly becoming the preferred drink among the nobility and the Church.

Within this context, commercial trade grew to vast extensions, leading to the creation of professional associations and specific trade routes. Commercial Europe awoke after a thousand years of fitful sleep and formed a regional sentiment that would shape local identities. The circulation of currency increased, products traveled great distances, and the desire to broaden trade routes and the known world paved the way for new discoveries yet to come.

Many of the merchants in major urban centers belonged to professional associations such as the Hanseatic League, an economic community that monopolized Baltic maritime trade. The League managed the exchange of products from the north, particularly skins, furs, wood, fish, metals, wax, honey, and amber, which it sold with the objective of obtaining other goods from the Near East, the Mediterranean, and the Orient, such as fabrics, salt, grain, and wine.

Many commercial conflicts were played out in the Mediterranean, especially among the Italian cities that dominated local exchange and part of the west-east navigation, which extended to the frontiers of the known world, tapering off along the Chinese Silk Route and other regions managed by western missionaries.

The merchant families of Venice and later Genoa marketed wines from the Italian Peninsula and the Aegean Sea islands, supplying cities such as Milan, Constantinople, and Krakow, and the region that is Sweden today. The wines from the south were sweeter and had a higher alcohol content, while those of the north were lighter and less alcoholic. This fact, along with a deficient system for storing wine, resulted in unstable products, which therefore had to be sold shortly after the fermentation process was completed. Their flavor, according to winemaker Miguel Torres Sr., would have been very close to vinegar:

The harvest began in September and ended in late October. In November the wines were quickly sold in European fairs for consumption during year-end festivals.

CHILEAN WINE. THE HERITAGE

"Table wines turned to vinegar very quickly due to their low alcohol level and because they were made with a complete lack of hygiene. In the best of cases they turned rancid."

Beer was the common beverage in what are today the Nordic countries, and in the majority of the cases it was made from malted oats. It was usually home-made to meet the needs of a family or a small group of people. Except for small quantities, beer was not a commercial product, due to its biological instability that impeded its storage, a problem that was not resolved until the 19th century, when Louis Pasteur made his discoveries in microbiology.

Grape harvests usually began in the early days of September and ended in late October. The resulting wines were quickly sold in numerous European fairs. Reasons for the rapid sale ranged from the characteristic instability of medieval wines to the desire to have fresh wine for the Christmas festivities to the need to ship them before the arrival of the dreaded winter storms. It was not unusual for wines from the eastern Mediterranean and Iberian Peninsula to reach northern Europe as late as the following August when the driest and lightest wines had already begun to turn to vinegar. In those years, France began to define itself as the wine capital of the world and England as its primary market. A growing concern for hygiene in the field of winemaking led to the wide-spread use of a practice introduced by the Dutch in which sulfur was burned to create sulfur dioxide as a disinfecting agent in wine-bearing vessels.

Due to its need to spread the Gospel and celebrate the holy mass, Christianity was responsible for the early development of medieval viticulture. Vine growing later became a peasant activity, and the constant need for labor contributed to the creation of new towns and villages. Wine therefore had a civilizing effect. It was not only a catalyst for trade, but an essential factor in the creation of new human settlements, as the vine is one of very few permanent crops that demand the constant attention of a trained workforce.

MODERN TIMES
Expansion and New Types of Wine

The Spanish brought the vine to the Americas, and it rapidly spread throughout the conquered territories. The first vineyards in the Viceroyalty of Peru were located near the Incan capital of Cuzco.

The urban and commercial development that took place in the late Middle Ages influenced the expansion and diversification of wine production. Agricultural progress, demographic increases, and navigational improvements motivated the search for new trade routes and communication with new markets. As a consequence, the wine industry generated major advances that would later be transferred to the American territories as they were conquered by the Europeans.

The New World was closely related to Europe, not only in political and cultural spheres, but in the adoption of wine during the process of the Conquest that shaped the new societies. The vine first arrived in the Americas during a historical period of expansion and change. The fall of the Eastern Roman Empire in charge of the Turkish Ottomans in 1453 was reflected in the introduction of the ancient knowledge and wisdom of the Byzantine scholars along the coasts of northeastern Italy. Some decades later, the Moors would be driven out of the Iberian Peninsula, strengthening the gradual fusion that was taking place in the Christian kingdoms.

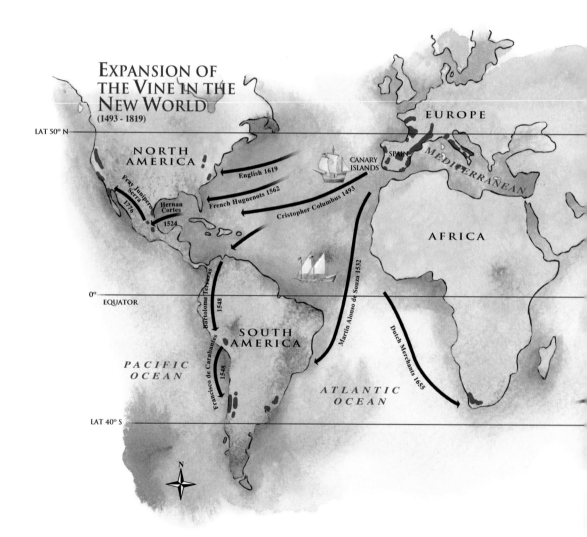

EXPANSION OF THE VINE IN THE NEW WORLD
(1493 - 1819)

LAT 50° N

NORTH AMERICA

EUROPE

SPAIN

MEDITERRANEAN

English 1619

CANARY ISLANDS

Fray Junipero Serra

1776

Hernan Cortes

1524

French Huguenots 1562

Cristopher Columbus 1493

AFRICA

0°
EQUATOR

Bartolome Terrazas

1548

Francisco de Carabantes

1548

SOUTH AMERICA

Martin Alonso de Souza 1532

Dutch Merchants 1655

PACIFIC OCEAN

ATLANTIC OCEAN

LAT 40° S

N

WINE IN THE NEW TERRITORIES

During Christopher Columbus' second voyage to the Americas in 1493, the Genovese mariner brought the first grapevine cuttings or seeds in order to introduce vine growing into the new territories conquered for "God and the King." The Spanish caravels entrusted *Vitis vinifera* with the double objective of propagating the Catholic faith and reducing the high costs of importing wines for consumption by the Spanish Conquistadors. The Spanish throne would support the introduction years later by enacting the 1522 ordinance that required all ships that departed for the New World to carry vine plants.

We know little about the way in which they were transported. It is assumed that at first they were cuttings and not grape seeds, because although the latter bore fruit without problems, the species' system of open pollination would have generated absolutely heterogeneous plants. There is no way of knowing with certainty the origin of the first European vines that reached the Americas.

Some historians and ampelographers defend the idea of Spanish origin, while others attribute them to the Canary Islands. The former believe that the Canary Islands would only have been an obligatory stop-over point on the voyage from Spain to the New World to assure the survival of the cuttings, while the latter believe that the vine had already been cultivated on the islands since the mid-15th century, after the Portuguese conquest of the territory in 1410.

Nevertheless, we know little about the early stages of development of the vine in the Americas, as there are no records of the nearly 30 years between

Columbus' second voyage in 1493, and 1524, when Hernán Cortés gave the order to plant vineyards in the Mexican highlands. It seems reasonable to believe that grape-growing attempts were unsuccessful given the inappropriate climatic and phytosanitary conditions of the newly-conquered lands. The abence of the vine in Central America can be explained to some degree by the region's tropical climate, although the possible presence of phylloxera may be a factor.

Hernán Cortés successfully introduced vines in the Mexican highlands, wich was possible because altitude attenuates the effects of the seasons, reduces relative humidity, and cools night temperatures, thus providing the day-night temperature differential that the vine needs. These conditions were essential for the vine to prosper in a latitude where the climate is semi-tropical and even tropical.

It is assumed that the vines that Cortés planted in Mexico were the variety known today as *Mission* in California, *País* in Chile, and *Criolla* in Argentina. The vines mutated over time and developed different clones, or sub-varieties, of a single variety, which is a common and natural characteristic of *Vitis vinifera sativa*, even over relatively short periods of time.

Columbus introduced the vine to the new territories "for God and the King" during his second trip to the Americas in 1493.

72

The Conquest soon expanded to South America, where Inca-controlled territories fell to a group of conquistadors led by Francisco Pizarro between 1532 and 1534, while Jiménez de Quezada and Pedro de Valdivia conquered Colombia and Chile respectively around 1541. We can deduce from those advances that the Spaniards planted vines with relative success in the territories around Cuzco, repeating a pattern similar to that of Mexico. However, sources indicate that Fray Bartolomé de Terrazas introduced the first vines in Peru in 1548, the same year that Fray Francisco de Carabantes brought vines to Chile.

The vast distances that separated the lands that are now Mexico and Peru, added to the difficulties of navigating the southern Pacific, presume the creation of strategies for decreasing the risks of transporting the vine and other European fruit stocks. It is very likely that the vines prospered earlier in the limited settlements of what is now Colombia and were later transferred to Peru in 1548.

There are different theories about the introduction of the vine in the provincial administration of Chile; the most probable suggests that Fray Francisco de Carabantes brought vines from Peru by sea to the current port of Talcahuano in early 1548, motivated by the need to have wine to celebrate the sacraments. Another theory held by some historians proposes that the vine arrived by horseback from Cuzco, across the arid Atacama Desert, although technically this would be difficult because the cuttings would have dehydrated and died during the 3,000-kilometer journey. We should also consider that vines have very delicate buds in their extremes, and once sprouted, they would have died due to the friction caused by the movement. Carabantes' mission would not have been much easier, because maritime connections were sporadic and rather risky during the early years of the Conquest, especially considering that between 1543 and 1545, ten of every fifty ships that sailed between Chile and Peru sank during the voyage.

In 1557, Fray Juan Cidrón transported vines across the Andes from the then recently-founded Chilean city of La Serena, due to the efforts of colonists from Santiago del Estero: Bartolomé de Mansilla, Nicolás Guernica, Hernán Macía Miraval, Pedro de Cáceres, and Rodrigo de Quiroga.

Not only the Spanish were involved in this vitivinicultural growth that took place within a context of commercial expansion and the opening of new maritime routes. The French Huguenots tried and failed to cultivate the vine in Florida between 1562 and 1564. In 1609 Lord Delaware tried again and was also unsuccessful. Despite their failure, the reference to those attempts is significant in that it is the first time that historians mention phylloxera and other diseases and pests as possible causes for the difficulties in planting vineyards in those lands.

It wasn`t until two centuries later that Franciscan priest Fray Junipero Serra laid the foundations of Californian vitiviniculture between 1770 and 1780 in the territory that belonged to the viceroyalty of New Spain, which later became Mexico.

The period of discoveries concluded toward the end of the 16th century, and the new mixed societies began to take shape. In this process, vine growing and wine production experienced a significant increase due to the presence of wineries not only in the new American territories, but also in South Africa, introduced by Dutch merchants around 1650. English colonists took vines to Australia in 1788 as part of an agricultural development plan to supply Great Britain with its own wine and to put an end to their dependency upon French wines.

Over the centuries, pre-Colombian America had maintained a state of isolation with respect to the European continent. This did not, however, prevent its inhabitants from creating formulas to produce alcoholic beverages derived from the fruit of the continent, such as the grapes indigenous to North America; *Vitis labrusca* and *Vitis berlandieri*, for example.

The American indigenous cultures incorporated alcohol into their diet and religious rituals, just as the early cultures of the Middle East and Europe had done many centuries earlier. We know that the first pre-Colombian alcoholic drinks came from breaking down and fermenting corn, and were generically known as *chicha*, a name derived from the Central American word used by a Panamanian tribe for corn, or maize: *chichab*. This term refers to a drink that is completely distinct from the Chilean drink of the same name, which is an alcoholic product made from the partial fermentation of grape must. Although the corn-based drink was one of the most common, others included *pulque*, prepared from *maguey* and *cahuín*.

In Chile, the fruits preferred by the indigenous people for making alcoholic drinks were native berries such as *maqui* (*Aristoltelia chilensis*), *molle* (*Schinus molle*), *huigán* (*Schinus polygamus*), and *murtilla* (*Ugni molinae*).

Women played a fundamental part in making these beverages; they chewed the grains and spit them into a container where the moisture of the saliva acted with the starch in the corn that caused it to break down and later ferment. Another technique was to grind the corn between stones and then add water.

However, that statement raises several questions, such as: what was the significance of introducing European wine to indigenous cultures? What developments followed? How was the vitivinicultural tradition of certain regions in the Americas forged?

The introduction of new guidelines for behavior, religious beliefs, political systems, eating habits, etc., provoked a rupture in the indigenous cultural system. One example was the arrival of European wine, which invited new standards for alcohol consumption, as it was not only related to religious rituals and festivities, but with daily village life as well. However, the high alcohol content in the wine distinguished it from autochthonous fruit-based beverages consumed previously and prepared by way of very dubious hygienic practices.

The introduction of wine had dramatic consequences that further increased with the consumption of distilled spirits known to the indigenous peoples since the arrival of Christopher Columbus. The new beverages had negative effects, not only because they interrupted a ritual of consumption related to religious practices, but also due to the physical effects generated by the high alcohol content. This phenomenon also occurred in North America with the introduction of distilled products that the natives called "fire water."

Indigenous peoples were familiar with alcoholic drinks made of corn and native berries prior to the conquest. The Spaniards introduced them to wine, grape chicha, and aguardiente.

In Chile the consequences were observed in psychological disorders, blindness, and other problems which, even now may be witnessed in the central south due to the effect of clandestinely-made *aguardientes* still available in the area.

These consequences invite a new look at the moral debt of the Spanish culture and the *huincas* (white men) to the indigenous population, especially with the series of stereotypes constructed around the drinking habits in the region. The natives soon learned the techniques of vitivinicultural production, prompting the Spaniards to establish regulations to this effect. Therefore, around 1579, Rodrigo de Quiroga, the Governor of Chile, announced that the *Indians* could not grow grapes because:

> *"...they make must and drink it, and then get so drunk that they kill each other ... I hereby publicly proclaim that within the next four months, all Indians who have vineyards and fig orchards on their lands must either pull out their vines by the roots or sell said vineyards and properties to Spaniards."*

The conflict caused by these early prohibitions gave rise to the much-feared "Drunkenness Judge," dreaded for the inhumane punishments he meted out for inebriation.

> *"One hundred lashes or the loss of all the containers of wine and beverages owned, and their heads shall be shaved, plus 50 lashes and a head shaving for each of the Indians (male or female) found drunk in or leaving a bar; this for the first offense, and for the second, the sentence will be doubled, or for the third, the sentence will be doubled plus ten days in the stocks."*

South America: the Provincial Administration of Chile

Fray Francisco de Carabantes introduced wine grapes to Chile in 1548 after finding it to be a paradise on Earth that would allow the grapes to grow and multiply easily. The plants were disembarked in the port of Talcahuano, although there is little record of where they were planted, how they were grown, or of any further links between the priest and viticulture.

The presence of this new plant species in the south of the Chilean territory is explained by the early importance of the Spanish settlement in Concepción as a base for the conquest of native Mapuche territory. Logic suggests that they must have planted some vines on the hills around the bay, but because the climate was colder than in the country's central zone, it is unlikely that the vines could have entered into production in less than four years. We can also assume that during his first trips to Santiago, Carabantes or his escorts transported vine cuttings to expand the crop. At least this is the suggestion of José Toribio Medina in his *Record of Tithes to the Episcopate (Memorial de los Diezmos del Obispado)*:

> *"Purchased from Alonso Moreno two jugs of wine to celebrate the mass (October 6, 1550). This was surely local wine, and we should disregard the possibility that Alonso Moreno's wine had been imported for the simple reason that the Church could also have made it and saved the markup that Alonso Moreno charged."*

Santiago of the New Extreme, founded on February 12, 1541, soon became Chile's political center. Its inhabitants – Spaniards, mestizos, and indigenous – all gathered around the Plaza Mayor, where they erected their homes, churches, and governmental offices. The Mapocho River bordered the settlement, and one of its branches, the Cañada, surrounded it, providing both protection and water thanks to pre-Colombian irrigation canals. The fertile lands that surrounded the city were soon put to use for gardens and vineyards in order to satisfy the basic needs of Santiago's inhabitants.

The earliest vitivinicultural productions would have taken place in Santiago, despite the fact that in his book *The First Grape Harvest in Chile* author Manuel Gandarillas placed the first harvest in 1556 by Francisco de Aguirre in Copiapó. This is possible in the sense of the first production, as prior vinifications had taken place in Santiago for local consumption and religious services. According to José Toribio Medina, Chilean wine's official birth certificate would have indicated Santiago, March 9, 1555, by Rodrigo de Araya.

The first vines in the valley of Santiago would have been planted in household gardens and along the banks of the Mapocho and the Cañada Rivers, which were set apart from the urban center where the majority of the population was concentrated. Alonso Moreno, Francisco de Montero, and Father Francisco González were involved in its commercialization in Santiago. In Valdivia, Father Luis Bonifacio was a leading figure, and in Concepción it was Juana Jiménez, another of Pedro de Valdivia's lovers and the niece of Inés de Suárez, the only Spanish woman to form a part of Pedro de Valdivia's Spanish army.

During the 16th century, most of the production of wine, *chicha*, and *aguardiente* originated in disperse household arbors in rural areas, where they shared space with other fruit trees, annual crops, and even cattle. At the turn of the century, the first regulations were set into place, requiring official authorization to plant new vineyards, which quickly produced a reduction in supply that impeded the ability to satisfy demand. This in turn prompted speculations, which were combated by the municipal authorities through the requisition of wines, *chichas,* and *aguardientes,* for later sale at fixed prices in established commercial centers, such as the Plaza Mayor or the Plaza de Armas.

Some years after Santiago was founded in 1541, the first wines were made at wineries along the banks of the Mapocho River, in the Maipo Valley.

CHILEAN WINE. THE HERITAGE

Water played an essential role in the development of the first vineyards; when they were planted at a distance from rivers or fertile lowlands, they depended upon artificial irrigation. In some areas, settlers inherited canals created by the indigenous cultures, while in other areas farmers built hydraulic works that eventually covered most of the area between the south of Santiago and Talca, modifying the face of the extensive brush land and "little Sahara," as Benjamín Vicuña Mackenna called it in his chronicles of the 18th century.

From this perspective, viticulture was massively developed only in the regions where rain was sufficiently copious and constant throughout the year. This then explains why although the first crops were in Santiago, La Serena, Copiapó, and all the northern irrigated areas, the true development took place in the south-central regions, such as Cauquenes and Mataquito, where the rain allowed the vine to grow without the need for artificial irrigation.

The first massive plantations consisted of head-trained vines, using the system inherited from Roman times and which still exists today in dry-farmed areas in the country's central south. These vineyards were located on hillsides, hillsides in accordance with the Spanish criteria that proposed leaving the less fertile lands for grapevines.

The plantations followed no uniform plan; plants rooted where they fell from the hand, and no precise records of their extension were kept. The few records that have reached our times refer to the number of vines planted, which allows us to deduce, with a high margin of error, that the surface area planted to vine at the end of the 18th century should have reached some 15,000 hectares, which is a high proportion in relation to the population. This production was gradually oriented not only to the internal market, but also to an export system managed by the viceroyalty of Peru, which commercialized approximately 40,000 *arrobas* of wine and 5,000 of *aguardiente*.

It is interesting to reflect upon the consequences that winegrowing had on the new territory. Not unlike the Medieval European context, Chilean vineyards acted as a factor that provided establishment to human settlements and the creation of new towns. In effect, there is a curious geographical line of dry-farmed lands that are apt for grape-growing that starts in San Francisco de Limache in the north, close to Valparaíso, and stretches south to the town of San Rosendo, east of Concepción.

Urban and rural communities interacted not only through the consumption and commerce of wine, but of *chicha* and *aguardiente* as well. The former was the favorite drink in colonial times, as it was considerably cheaper than wine and more pleasant than *aguardiente*. Chilean *chicha*, which is very similar to the sweet wines of the Middle Ages and ancient times, was produced in specific places where they heated the must to concentrate it. Once the first fermentation was finished, the product was stored in large clay jugs called *tinajas*, where it began a slow and continuous phenomenon of fermentation that gave rise to *chicha cocida* or cooked *chicha*.

Chicha consumption also had its socio-economic impact. The large clay *tinajas* in which it was made were almost impossible to move, and therefore the consumers were forced to move to obtain it, thus creating a type of denomination of origin that characterizes the production in different parts of the country, that holds even to today, for example, *chicha* from areas such us Villa Alegre, Curacaví, and Quilicura.

Chicha was distinguished not only by its denomination of origin, but by grape variety as well. Despite the sources that mention varieties such as *Dedos de Dama*, *Cocos de Gallo*, and *San Francisco*, it is difficult to find these varieties today because the only pre-19th century varieties that have reached our times on an industrial scale are *País* and *Moscatel de Alejandría*. The previously-mentioned colonial varieties may actually be those now found in home arbors that produce good table grapes.

Colonial vinification techniques produced an unstable product that was difficult to transport. Even more difficult was the distillation process that resulted in a rather noxious aguardiente harmful to human health due to the precarious conditions of production. Paradoxically, this was one of the most-consumed beverages in colonial times, and it was not until the late 19th century that wine became a product of mass consumption of wine in Chile.

The development of vitiviniculture during the colonial period was gradual, slow, and difficult, and it was rare to find large extensions of land dedicated exclusively to wine grape production.

It is important to point out, however, that the quantity and quality of wine produced in Chile was motive for admiration for the few European visitors of the times, two hundred years before California and earlier than any other country of the southern hemisphere. The references to this are too numerous to name, but one example was written by British Admiral Byron in his travelogue, *Journey Around the World*, published in 1758, in which he says:

> *"The estancias or country homes are very picturesque and usually have beautiful olive groves and vineyards. In my opinion, Chilean wine is as good as that of Madeira".*

Across the Andes: the Vine in the Viceroyalty of La Plata

The first grapevines were brought to Santiago del Estero in 1557 from La Serena by Fray Juan Cidrón. Other historians maintain that the plants came from an expedition undertaken by Diego de Rojas in 1542 and that the first vineyards were planted by the Guanacache Lagoon, formed by the Mendoza and San Juan Rivers, fluvial sources that would later have great importance in the development of vitiviniculture in the Cuyo region. In those years, according to data from Juan López de Velasco, the region of Cuyo consisted of 150 Spaniards and 4,000 natives who worked the large plantations.

The first vines would have arrived in the future cities of San Juan and Mendoza with the Chilean vitivinicultural pioneer, merchant, and conquistador Juan Jufré when he founded the city of San Juan in 1561, accompanied by his lieutenants Mallea, Ahumada, Contreras, and Marqués.

While the vine entered the Cuyan territories, the region of Río de la Plata, with a larger concentration of residents and commercial trade in Buenos Aires, was forced to refrain from commercial vine production for climatic reasons. After the early days of the Conquest and forging the colonial society, the Spaniards began to change their perception of Cuyo. Travelers and merchants reported the abundant harvests of fruit, grapes, wheat, and other agricultural products. During a 1641 visit to Mendoza, Chilean Jesuit Alonso de Ovalle praised the area in the following terms:

> "The land is very abundant in bread, wine, meat, vegetables, and every kind of European fruit, especially almond and olive groves… This area supplies the entire provincial administration of Tucuman to Buenos Aires and Paraguay with figs, raisins, pomegranates, peaches, apples, olives, and abundant quantities of very good wine, which they ship throughout the pampas."

Referring to Cuyan wines, he said:

> "They are very generous and so strong that they can travel over land more than three or four hundred leagues through the intense heat of the Tucuman and Buenos Aires pampas, by oxen, on journeys that last many months without sustaining any damage, and then they last as long as desired without spoiling, and in such abundance, that they supply all the territory and provinces, even as far away as Paraguay."

This agricultural and industrial development generated an increase in wine production, and 120 vineyards were registered in Mendoza in 1739, within a range of a mere 66 hectares. The crop extended to other regions, reaching as far as Cordoba and Salta in the north, but communicational difficulties and the enormous distances were factors that impeded commercial trade between the coastal cities and the interior. During the 18th century, vineyard plantations in the Cuyo region maintained and increased their prestige, as was noted by Damián Hudson and Bishop José Aníbal Verdaguer, increasing commercial trade that was becoming increasingly important.

Tales of travelers such as Haencke tell of the abundance of grapes in the houses of Mendoza and the custom of producing raisins and conserving them for the winter. This traveler also adds that Mendoza's wines and aguardientes were not inferior to those of Andalucia, "...*in both their good qualities and their extraordinary abundance.*" However, it wasn't until the arrival of the railroad in the 19th century that the interior was connected with the large coastal cities, giving rise to a commercial development that increased wine production considerably. Along with advances in transportation mediums, wine containers were also modified, and the original reed-lined clay vessels were replaced with wooden barrels and casks in the late 18th century.

Fray Juan Cidrón carried grapevines across the Andes Mountains from La Serena, Chile to Santiago del Estero, Argentina, in 1557.

CHILEAN WINE. THE HERITAGE

The Viceroyalty of Peru

There are various theories about the grapevine's arrival in Peru. While Father Bernabé Cobo wrote that the first vines were planted in the city of Lima by order of Hernando de Montenegro and provided their first grapes in 1551, Garcilaso de la Vega claims that Fray Bartolomé de Terrazas introduced grapevines even earlier and first vinified in 1560. Inca Garcilaso claims that this took place at the Marcahuasi Hacienda, property of Pedro López de Gazalla, who yearned more for the honor and fame attached to being the first to make wine from his own vineyards, than for the economic benefits.

Despite the difficulties in establishing the origins, vine growing extended throughout the viceroyalty and was particularly concentrated in the region of Ica (300 kilometers south of Lima), which initiated Peruvian viticulture. As the economic and political center during the first centuries of the Colony, Peru monopolized commerce between Spain and South America and directed the exchange between its dependent territories. This exchange depended upon the regulations imposed by the crown, which sought to privilege Spanish winemakers and thus theoretically limit the production of wine in the viceroyalties and provincial administrations. In practice, these restrictions were often ignored, which explained the 100 ships that left Lima each year to sell Peruvian wine in the American colonies.

In the 17th century, Spain imposed a number of restrictions that affected the development of vitiviniculture in its American colonies. The Crown was not oblivious to the increase in production and at one time prohibited Peruvian wine from entering Guatemala and Panama, where the Spanish fleet arrived to trade with the colonies.

The Portuguese Colony of Brazil

The vine reached the Portuguese colony of Brazil before it arrived in Peru and Chile. In 1532 Martin Alonso de Souza introduced the vine in the province of Sao Vicente on the southern coast of Brazil, although the Brazilians designated Bras Cubas, founder of the city of Santos, as their first winegrower. He produced the first wines around 1551 in the region of Tatuape, in the town of Sao Paulo do Campo. Other references indicate that around 1625, Jesuit missionary Roque Gonzalez de Santa Cruz introduced wine in the extreme south of Brazil, primarily as a part of the Christian liturgy, by founding the San Nicolau Christian Reservation along the Uruguay River. Vine growing never achieved economic importance in Brazil and has largely remained a crop for household use.

The Viceroyalty of New Spain: Mexico

The configuration of New Spain as one of the greatest political powers of the colonial Americas stimulated agricultural development. Vine growing was encouraged by the authorities, as is illustrated by the order given by Hernán Cortés on March 20, 1524:

> *"Anyone having dependent Indians is hereby obligated to proportionally plant a minimum of one thousand grape vines each year, even though they be plants of your own land, until reaching the allotted number of five thousand vines."*

Cortés' order reveals the importance of the vine and the need for wine produced within the colonial territories. He also provides interesting technical solutions, and we can deduce that the propagation method used by the Spaniards was grafting, because he suggests *"grafting the European varieties to those of the land."* With this phrase Cortés encouraged grafting *Vitis vinifera sativa* over American *Vitis*, thereby recommending the association of the two species, a technique that was not massively employed in Europe until the 19th century when the vineyards were threatened by the scourge of phylloxera. This ensured vitivinicultural activity in the Americas through the use of grafting some 350 years prior to Europe's desperate 15-year search for a solution to the destruction caused by phylloxera.

Hernán Cortés introduced grapevines to the Viceroyalty of Mexico in the early 16th century, grafting Vitis vinifera sativa vines onto American rootstocks, anticipating the solution that would resolve Europe's phylloxera crisis centuries later.

The early colonial years were dedicated to stabilizing vine growing and winemaking. Toward the end of the 18th century, missionaries produced their own wines in the missions in northern Mexico, San Diego, San Juan de Capistrano, San Buenaventura, San Gabriel, and Santa Barbara, as well as in Carlos, Soledad, San Antonio, San Luis Obispo, and Santa Clara. Viticulture never reached a significant level farther south, thereby precluding wine from the daily diet of the Mexican people and presaging the low per capita consumption it would have over the coming centuries.

Northeastern United States

The travelogues of seafarers and explorers, as well as the manuscripts housed in Norwegian and Danish libraries tell of the Viking journeys to the American continent. One particularly impressive account relates the story of Leif Eriksson, son of Eric the Red, in 1000 AD and his journey to what is now northeastern Canada. This adventure, as told by Adolph Cornau in America in 1892, could confirm that *Vitis vinifera sativa* once existed in America and was later destroyed by phylloxera.

> *"One day, one of the explorers failed to return to his colleagues. He was a Teuton named Thyrker. Leif and twelve men set out to search for him. When they found him he was very excited and quickly told them that he had seen large numbers of grapevines, which he knew perfectly well from his homeland. The mariners set to work at two tasks. First they loaded their ships and then picked all the grapes they could, filling a large boat. When the spring came, they returned to Greenland with their cargo. Leif called this country Vinland."*

Toward the 16th century, the territory now occupied by the United States continued to be seen as a frontier land seemingly somewhere between legend and fiction. The area essentially consisted of the Atlantic coast, where phylloxera was the lord of the land and soil.

The first attempts to introduce *Vitis vinifera sativa* failed, as phylloxera, oidium, and powdery mildew put a quick end to them. Along with the failures in Florida and Virginia, Spaniards were making progress planting in what is now Paris Island, off the coast of South Carolina. Due to the constant problems with *Vitis vinifera*, grape growers had their first viticultural successes with the indigenous species *Vitis labrusca* and *Vitis rotundfolia*. They also crossed *labrusca* with *vinifera sativa*, thus generating new species called hybrids or direct producers. Sources report that a French Protestant colony along the St. John River in Fort Caroline, Florida produced sufficient Moscatel wine to fill 20 barrels in 1564, although it wasn't until the late 18th century that Mexicans and Spaniards began to develop a continuous and massive wine industry based on *Vitis vinifera sativa* in California.

Beyond the Americas: South Africa

The history of South African vitiviniculture began when the Dutch settled in the Cape of Good Hope. Three years later, in 1655, Jean Van Riebeeck, the first governor of the colony, planted a vineyard. On February 2, 1659, he wrote of the first harvest in his diary:

> *"Today, praised be the Lord, the must of the grape was pressed for the first time in the Cape."*

His successor was Simon Van der Stel, who worked diligently to improve vitivinicultural production, which around 1672 allowed for the distillation of the Cape's first brandy. In the late 17th century, a group of French Huguenots escaping from religious persecution arrived in the region. They had good knowledge of the techniques and methods used in the vineyards of France and therefore contributed to the progress of the culture of wine in South Africa.

The famous dessert wine Vin de Constance was created some years later and exported to Europe with great success. The region of Constantia was the birthplace of South African wine and even today it is renowned for its white wine production.

NEWS FORMS FOR WINE

The colonization of new territories extended Europe's commercial market, promoting trade and the intensification of the lands under vine. Behind this agricultural expansion, dietary improvement, and increase in the European population, there was a series of technological advances that promoted the increase in production, thereby providing a foundation for the gradual shift from feudal economy to budding capitalism. Commercial expansion implied profound transformations in agriculture and the incipient industry, imparting an increasing strength and significant weight to agricultural development as a source of income. The closed economy inherited from the 14th century began its globalization phase toward the end of the 18th century, renewing the operative mechanisms for trade. Systems of credit became easier and the bank draft arose as the common mercantile instrument, developing multiple procedures and practices that allowed for the expansion of commerce into different countries. This produced a fundamental change in the existing vitiviniculture, as it originated new types of wine and improved distilled spirits according to the tastes of foreign consumers, promoting the early development of agro-industry.

Distilled Spirits

While a new cultural order born of European inheritance and crossbreeding (*mestizaje*) took hold in the Americas, experimentation with wine continued in the Old Continent. The introduction of the alembic still in its "industrial" form by the Moors of the Iberian Peninsula promoted distillation processes. The still, however, presents a connection with the Greeks, which coincides with the ideas of some researchers who assert that the Greeks and Romans were the first to employ still-like devices.

During the Middle Ages, the distillation process played a prevailing role for the alchemists and sorcerers in the creation of beverages that contained alcohol. Little by little its medical uses were spread through the work of learned men such as Ramón Llull (1233-1315) of Mallorca, and Arnaldo de Vilanoba of Valencia, who used it to modify the alcohols known in medicine for therapeutic purposes, such as aquavit. However, despite its existence since the 13th century, pure alcohol was not sold as such until 200 years later. Although it could only be legally obtained for use as a medicinal beverage, its consumption became popular through fraudulent means. Given its increasing demand as a drink in the late 15th century, the first alcohol laws were put into place in 1493, thus prompting the birth of the alcohol industry. A wide assortment of beverages began to appear based on alcohol derived from products that contained sugar and starch. For example, grains were used as their starches can be broken down into sugar and fermented, followed by a distillation process to generate the desired alcohol. Although it was relatively easy to obtain alcohol by these methods, it continued to be difficult to produce alcohol that was good, safe, and pleasing to the palate.

Distilled spirits are distinguished by the quantities and characteristics of the impurities that they contain because pure ethyl alcohol is chemically identical, regardless of its origin. These impurities formed by tiny amounts of esters, aldehydes, superior alcohols, and traces of methyl alcohol have variable proportions and characteristics, supplied by the basic origins of the alcohol, the different processes of distillation, and aging in different types of wood, etc. These characteristics make it possible to distinguish between cognac, pisco, whisky, and other spirits. Achieving flavors that differ so widely from one spirit to the next depends upon the raw ingredients used, the way in which the process is conducted, and the type of aging the product undergoes, including both the time it is aged and the type of container used. The way distilled spirits are made therefore varies according to the idiosyncrasies and customs of the makers. The commercialization of distilled spirits meant a strong competition for the vitivinicultural industry. Furthermore, spirits have certain advantages over wines in terms of stability and durability, characteristics that were highly valued in the European market, which still suffered sanitary and preservation problems in transporting their products.

The Moors introduced the alembic still to the Iberian Peninsula and promoted the process of distillation. The words 'alcohol' and 'alembic' have Arabic roots and are derived from the words al-Koh'l and al'ambiq.

CHILEAN WINE. THE HERITAGE

Armagnac

Armagnac originated in the French province of Gascony, birthplace of Musketeer D'Artagnan of Alejandro Dumas' famous novel, the Three Musketeers. The character was based on Charles de Batz, lord of the Castelmore Castle, whose descendent, the Marquis de Montesquieu, Duke of Fezensac, is considered to be the creator of armagnac. This spirit, France's oldest brandy, was born of two cultures: the Romans, who introduced vine growing, and the Moors, who expanded the use of the alembic still. This beverage was first produced around the year 1300 for use in alchemy. It wasn't until 300 years later that it became an important commercial product. It is based on wine made from Gascony-grown grapes, particularly Ugni Blanc, Colombard, and Folle Blanche, and is distilled just once, very slowly, using the alembic still, which reached its definitive shape just 150 years ago.

Cognac

History attributes the creation of Cognac to the 17th century French nobleman, Sir de la Croix Marron. In an attempt to claim grandeur and capture the soul of the brandy he distilled it a second time, obtaining what we know today as Cognac. After distilling the wine directly, he introduced the result to a second distillation process known as *deuxième chauffe* or *bonne chauffe*. The process was improved over time, and distillation and ageing techniques were developed and strictly regulated. Cognac begins with completely neutral wines made from grape varieties Folle Blanche, Ugni Blanc and Colombard. The wine is distilled and the resulting spirit is later aged in barrels for a distinctive amber color and a complex bouquet.

Brandy

The word brandy comes from a transformation of the Dutch word *brandwijn*, which means *burnt wine*. The creator of the term is believed to be a 17th-century Dutch traveler who wanted to facilitate the transportation of wine by employing a common technique of the time based on a simple distillation that produced common spirits.

The product was also called *Holland* for its origin. In 1875, thanks to the intervention of the Spanish company Pedro Domecq, and practically by accident, it was discovered that ageing the product in noble barrels produced spirits as good as cognac, prompting the Spanish to adopt the expression coñac. Today in Spain this spirit is called brandy rather than coñac due to the opposition of French Minister of Agriculture Hennesy, who stood behind a protectionist law passed in 1928.

Pisco

Pisco is a wine based *aguardiente,* or distilled spirit, that began in the Americas in the mid-16th century after the grapevine and distillation processes were introduced by the Spaniards. The name derives from the Quechua word *pishkos* that referred to the small birds that flocked over the area now known as the port of Pisco in Southern Peru. This expression was first used for the town, then the containers produced there, and finally the spirit that was sold in them.

The first regions to generate Pisco in the Americas were Chile and Peru, where it became a popular drink for the former and an emblematic beverage for the latter, where its consumption competed with distilled cane spirits.

In Peru the areas traditionally oriented to Pisco production and that currently have an Apellation or Denomination of Origin (D.O.) are the departments of Lima, Ica, Arequipa, and Moquegua, along with the Locumba, Sama, and Caplina Valleys in Tacna. Peruvian Pisco is obtained primarily by distilling wine made from the non-aromatic Quebranta grape, introduced during the Conquest, along with other varieties such as Moscatel de Alejandría, Torontel, and Italia.

Peruvian Pisco has traditionally been made through an artisanal process by hundreds of small producers; in recent decades, however, a few plants with industrial technologies have been added to the fold. There are four types of Pisco in Peru, characterized by their varied aromatic potential: Pure Pisco (Quebranta, Mollar, and Negra Corriente), Aromatic Pisco (Moscatel, Italia, Albilla, and Torontel), Acholado Pisco (blend of varieties), and Mosto Verde Pisco (distilled from half-fermented musts).

Chile's Pisco tradition dates back to the 17th and 18th centuries, particularly to the Coquimbo area, where rustic stills and ancient troughs can still be found today. The D.O. is reserved for *aguardiente* made in the "Pisco Zone", which is limited to the III and IV regions, specifically the Copiapó, Choapa, Elqui, and Limarí Valleys. The particular combination of temperature and luminosity in these areas favors the grape varieties used for this spirit, such as Moscatel de Austria, Moscatel Rosada, Moscatel de Alejandría, Torontel, and Pedro Jiménez. The industry was modernized in the 20th century, and the production processes were modified to improve quality and increase volumes.

Whisky

Although whisky, which is made from grain, rather than grapes, leads us away from the area of wine, it is interesting as a competitor. It is made through three steps: malting, fermentation, and distillation.

Despite its uncertain origins, it is believed to have begun in Scotland in 1495 and intensified around 1655, when it became one of the world's most prestigious distilled spirits. It was in even greater demand in the 20th century. Scotch whisky can only be produced in Scotland, where it is closely tied to long tradition. Water, the basis of all good distillates, is filtered through thick layers of Scottish peat and then used to moisten the barley, which is spread out in layers of no more than 60 cm (about 2 feet), germinating, and resulting in a product called green malt. The grain is then separated from its shoots and placed in peat-fueled kilns to dry at temperatures of no more than 70°C (158°F). The sugars are released during this stage. The malted grain is then ground and submerged in hot water. The thick product obtained is stirred for several hours to achieve a new liquid called "wort," which is then transferred to fermenting tanks that produce the wash, which is only 5% alcohol. The first distillation results in a clear liquid called "low wine," while the second distillation produces whisky with a concentration of approximately 58%. This concentration is reduced before placing the whisky in oak barrels, where it must age for a minimum of three years before it can be sold.

New Wines

The appreciation of the new alcoholic beverages that originated in the distillation process encouraged further research into winemaking in Europe. There were two fundamental problems that concerned researchers: how to maintain the connection between the source (grapes) and the final product (the wine they produced) and how to achieve the incorruptibility of the wines. The latter was extremely difficult because hygienic processes were unknown, as was the existence of microbiological agents that affected the stability of the wines. One of the first investigations concentrated on fortified wines, which have a higher alcohol (15-23%). This is achieved either by adding wine-based alcohol after fermentation or because the original must contains so much sugar that the product reaches a higher degree of alcohol without having to add further alcohol artificially.

Fortified Wines

Tradition holds that the famous Tokay wines were obtained accidentally, as the wars that devastated Hungary in the 17th century obligated a delay in harvests. The result was that the grapes destined for winemaking had become raisins and were affected by the noble rot caused by *Botrytis cinerea*, a fungus that causes a natural concentration of sugar in the grapes.

The result of the fermentation process was a particularly sweet fortified wine. Pliny had previously referred to *diachyton*, a wine made from bunches that were cut and left to dry for seven days, which produced the concentration of sugar necessary to produce sweet wine. These techniques were distributed around the world through artisanal recipes that had certain steps in common.

Those wines received different names. In Chile it was associated with Cauquenes, where it was called *asoleado* (sun-baked); the Germans called it *Spätlese* (from grapes that have over-ripened on the vine), and *Eiswein* in the north (from frozen grapes). Versions from southern Europe include Malvasia from Rhodes, and the Italian Albana and Vin Santo.

Sherry and Port

Toward the end of the 16th century, the Spanish offered wines they called *vinicoci* or *cooked wines*, obtained from musts that were concentrated through heat and then added to normal wines for greater stability and giving rise to the product that was to become Jerez (Sherry). In England it was first called sherry-sack, and then quickly shortened to its current name, sherry.

The 17th century was a time of defining the celebrated fortified and dry wines such as the Spanish Sherry, which was aged in oak barrels, and the Portuguese Port, which employed chestnut casks.

These wines had alcohol added and were mixed with small portions of naturally sweet wines or concentrated musts that gave them characteristic smells and colors. These wines also included air contact in their ageing process by leaving the surface area exposed, thus generating a thick soup of yeast that gave the wine very peculiar gustatory and olfactory characteristics. These principles continue today, essentially without variation.

Champagne

In addition to being one of the most original forms of wine, Champagne is also lively and effervescent. Its history is full of anecdotes that blend fact with fiction, beginning in late 17th-century France, when religious orders began to produce high-quality wines.

The grape varieties available in the district of Champagne, 150 kilometers northeast of Paris, tended to produce highly acidic, low alcohol white wines. A Benedictine abbey in Hautvillers was home to a blind monk named Dom Pérignon, and stories tell of his wisdom and patience along with a privileged palate accentuated by his blindness.

He is said to be not only the first to use a bottle and cork for wine, but also the creator of the beverage we know today as champagne, a discovery that caused him to shout, *"Come quickly! I'm drinking stars!"* His creation became the symbol of the region, a statue was erected in his memory, and an annual wine festival is organized by the people of Hautvillers.

Champagne is made from three varieties: Pinot Noir, Chardonnay, and to a lesser degree, Pinot Meunier. Once the wine is obtained, sugar is added in very specific proportions along with yeasts that are specially adapted to survive in the wine's high alcohol content.

The palate of French monk Dom Pérignon was exacerbated by his blindness. When he tasted the creation that would make him famous, he cried out, "Come quickly! I'm drinking stars!"

It is quickly bottled, and based on the added sugar and the little oxygen that remains in the bottle, the yeast begins a long, slow, second fermentation that lasts three or four months. During this time the carbon dioxide is reincorporated into the wine, giving rise to Champagne's characteristic bubbles. This second fermentation, which has been defined as the incorporation of one wine within another, generates small quantities of lees that are eliminated during the long one-to-two-year ageing process.

The bottles are placed upside-down in racks to begin the delicate process of riddling, whereby the lees settle into the neck of the bottle. They are then ready for disgorgement; the bottle necks are quickly frozen before opening the bottles, and the sediments are rapidly expelled by the force of the compressed carbon dioxide contained within. A sweet mixture of wine and sugar (dosage) is added and the bottle is quickly stoppered with a champagne cork. Depending on the amount of sugar in the dosage, the final product will be labeled Nature (without sugar), Brut (very little sugar), and Sec, Demi Sec, and Doux, with increasingly greater amounts of residual sugar.

The rapid acceptance of this beverage encouraged its production in new regions and the French defense of the term Champagne. The Germans call it *sekt*; the Spanish agreed in the 20th century to call their own version *cava*, while Chile just recently acquiesced to the European Union and will stop using the term in 2008 in international markets and 2015 internally.

BOTTLES AND CORKS: THE ALLIES OF FINE WINE

Although the Egyptians worked with glass more than 4000 years ago and cork stoppers were marginally known to the Romans, their use in wine is relatively recent. During the first centuries of the Christian era, work was begun with blown glass. This technique allowed the production of small bottles, glasses, and other receptacles. With the passage of time and the beginning of the Middle Ages, its use extended to the pharmaceutical area and in approximately 1650 to the wine industry. It is believed that the first wine bottle was fabricated in 1657 for the King's Head Tavern in Oxford, England.

Taverns then began ordering their own bottles as the wine producers did not supply them until much later. Another important tavern was the Pontac's Head in London, property of Arnaud de Pontac, president of the Bordeaux parliament. This tavern marketed and distributed Pontac Wine from the vineyard known today as Château Haut-Brion.

The first bottles were flat and unmanageable and were modified in the early 18th century to a cylindrical shape similar to that used today. The diverse origins of European wines allowed for the development of different bottle shapes, particularly the classical Bordeaux and Burgundy forms. The latter was the common cylindrical, high-shouldered, dark or light green bottle used primarily for Bordeaux reds such as Cabernet Sauvignon, Merlot, Carmenère, and Cot (Malbec). Clear bottles were also used for the region's white wines, such as Sauvignon Blanc. The Burgundy bottle, also cylindrical, was much wider and had lower, softly-sloping shoulders used for its wines based on Chardonnay and Pinot Noir.

Early bottles made it possible to identify the wines and differentiate their quality. Their shapes were modified to allow for better aging.

Chile once used the Alsatian or hock bottle, though its use gradually decreased. Other bottle shapes include the franconia or bocksbeutel, intended for white wines, although they've also been used for red wines in Chile and Portugal. The attractive shapes of wine bottles is not only due to aesthetic appeal, but also to the happy coincidence between the afore-mentioned functionality and beauty, one more expression of the distinguished atmosphere that always accompanies wine.

The use of cork to seal bottles was widespread by the late 17th century. Some credit Fray Dom Pérignon with the rediscovery of its usefulness in wine bottles, thus giving rise to an irreplaceable symbiosis between the cork and the bottle, despite the passage of time and technological changes. Cork comes from the bark of the cork tree, *Quercus suber*, which is similar to oak and grown on the Iberian Peninsula. The tree must be at least twenty years old before its cork can be cut for the first time, and it can then be harvested every eight years thereafter to obtain the raw material used to make cork stoppers. The last decade has seen the appearance of synthetic closures that comply with the function of a cork to a certain extent. At the beginning of the 21st century, major wineries in Europe and Chile have replaced the natural cork with metal screw caps similar to those long used for distilled spirits. It is doubtful that the cork will disappear, however, as its association with wine and the bottle is tightly linked in the minds of consumers, as is its usefulness in storage.

Bordeaux bottles have high, pronounced shoulders, which helped contain the sediments, while Burgundy bottles have sloping shoulders.

Bottles should be stored horizontally so that the cork remains in contact with the wine and mist. Good quality corks can last as long as fifteen years, and if the wine is to be stored longer, the cork should be changed.

Cork- and bottle-making have shifted from craft to industry, and together they provide a hermetic closure that allows essential biochemical processes necessary for the development of fine wines. As previously stated, the final process of ageing fine wine should take place in an environment as close to oxygen-free as possible. This can be achieved through an aesthetic, practical, and functional container, such as the glass bottle. On the other hand, the only closure capable of generating these conditions is the cork, which is elastic, resistant, impermeable, long-lived, and chemically stable. Therefore, the combination of bottle and cork is not only useful from the mechanical perspective, but to date it is the only way known to ensure that the wine develops in a reliable reductive environment.

Inside the bottle, the wine's aldehydes, esters, ketones, and fatty acids remain constant evolution, giving rise to the bouquet, or tertiary aromas. Primary aromas, which pertain directly to the grape, plus the secondary aromas from the fermentation process, and the bouquet, comprise what some authors define as the aromatic profile. Thus the wine matures and evolves from a wine with young, fruity, and floral aromas to one with mature aromas, such as coffee, musk, and many other complex organic aromas.

THE CONTEMPORARY ERA IN THE OLD WORLD

The Vitivinicultural Industry

In 1853, Nathaniel Rothschild acquired the Château Brane-Mouton winery in Medoc, in northern Bordeaux. It was later named a premier cru in 1973.

After the urbanization process that took place in Europe around 1500 and the period of development that followed the conquest of the Americas, a slow pace settled in that lasted 200 years. Stimulated by the accumulation of knowledge and inventions, progress reached different productive sectors in the mid-18th century, influencing both the general way of life and technological advances in production and communication processes.

The Industrial Revolution in Great Britain, the Netherlands, Switzerland, and France unleashed an accelerated pattern of growth that would turn Europe into the world leader of technological advancement. Europe's population doubled, encouraging the development of urban life, and greater food consumption motivated improvements in the nascent agro-industry. New tools made agricultural work easier, while the use of fertilizers improved the productivity of the soil.

Another interesting factor was the increasing specialization in food production resulting from the modernization of transportation systems. This allowed an increase in the product quality and the rise of sustained regional economies based on the production of specific items. The larger number of consumers stimulated an increase in the demand for wine and necessitated the search for more productive vines, neglecting the aspects inherent in the quality of the product. The substantial improvement of land, river, and maritime communication between the large cities allowed winegrowers in distant areas to risk competition in those markets, resulting in the conversion of a considerable extension of crop lands to vineyards. This fierce competition motivated producers from traditional viticultural areas, such as Bordeaux and Burgundy, to generate protective strategies and gave rise to the foundations of a future denomination of origin.

With the generalized use of bottles and corks in the 18th century came the concept of a winery as an entity; prior to that time wine had only been identified by its geographic origin. The change spawned a hierarchy that differentiated between the producers of high quality wines and those who made 'common' wines, particularly from the Gamay variety, used for the majority of the population. Wine production in the 19th century was characterized by three fundamental landmarks: the use of chaptalization, the outstanding contributions of Louis Pasteur and his research on the stability of wine, and the appearance of phylloxera and other diseases. The latter provoked a crisis of enormous dimensions, which, in the case of France, resulted in a monumental set-back from which it was unable to recover completely until the mid-20th century.

New Industry Practices

Industrialization and an increase in population and urban development, generated an increase in the demand for wine, which was difficult to satisfy. Winegrowers, farmers, and merchants introduced new practices and processes to revitalize vitivinicultural production in the European regions. The adulteration of time-honored enological recipes was so frequent that it finally had to be regulated. The use of colorants, inadequate clarification of the wine, and the introduction of fruit juices along with the grapes affected not only the consumers, but a product that had formerly maintained its high prestige in the European culture for centuries.

Chaptalization: the Enological use of Sugar

Jean Antoine Chaptal was born in 1766, twenty-three years before the French Revolution. He studied chemistry at Montpellier University, was a professor in Paris, an important enologist, a political figure and Napoleon Bonaparte's Minister of the Interior in 1800. One of his major scientific achievements links him to winemaking, as he is credited with discovering the importance of sugar in fermentation and the process of adding sugar to must to increase the amount of alcohol achieved in the future wine. Chaptal was not the first however, to use this type of methodology – there are records indicating that Nicolas Bidet, Simon Maupin, and one Abbot Rosier had used sugar to modify the alcohol content in their wines in the late 18th century. But the process came to be known as chaptalization due to the importance of Chaptal's scientific contributions made to education and renovating ancient vitivinicultural practices.

The introduction of these new possibilities in the process of wine production has always provoked controversies, as in many regions it is considered a falsification of the natural conditions of the vine and the grape. In the beginning, chaptalization was used primarily in those countries with cold climates that impeded the complete ripening of the grape, using cane or beet sugar to increase the potential alcohol content. However, its use in France was only legalized in 1929, when the practice was officially accepted north of Bordeaux and Côte du Rhone, where its use had apparently been widespread. Vitivinicultural legislation in other countries, such as Chile, considers chaptalization to be a falsification; however, the image and prestige of French wine is so well positioned that the use of this technique is usually overlooked as one of those well-kept family secrets, only known by the patriarchs. The process of enriching the wine is considered negative as incorporating fermentable agents such as cane sugar in place of grape musts acts against the purity of the product.

Louis Pasteur: a Radical Change in the Concept of Winemaking

The renowned biochemist and bacteriologist Louis Pasteur (1822-1895) was responsible for major advances in the beer industry through pasteurization, a method that applies extreme temperature fluctuations to food products without altering their basic characteristics. This process destroys bacteria, yeast, and other germs, thereby achieving the desired stability. By instruction of Emperor Luis Napoleon, Pasteur was required to apply his major findings in the dairy and wine industries in addition to his contributions to medicine.

Pasteur had already been recognized for demonstrating and explaining the phenomenon of fermentation prior to showing that yeasts generate a leavening action that initiated the process. Those discoveries, which established the basis of what we now know as enological chemistry, resolved many of the problems derived from the lack of hygiene in winemaking. His discoveries also revealed the efficacy of sanitary measures in preventing the action of microorganisms that decomposed the wine, thereby reducing the frequent use of chemical agents that were harmful to human health, such as fluoride and salicylic acid. There is no doubt that Louis Pasteur's greatest contribution was the practical management of winemaking and ageing by applying preventative rather than curative hygienic criteria, thereby finally producing the desired stability of wines that had been sought after for more than 3,000 years.

Louis Pasteur's studies led to finding the desired stability in wine. His research emphasized the importance of asepsis in the productive chain, a factor that became the basis for future winemaking.

Today's preventative measures are largely facilitated by current installations and procedures, where the use of stainless steel tanks and pipelines is essential. In sum, the discovery of the microbiological pathogens responsible for the problems allowed the comprehension of the importance of asepsis throughout the entire winemaking chain, thereby forming the cornerstone of future vine management and the industrial development of vitiviniculture of the last century.

Enemies of the Vine

Wine's new-found success, as a result of the new discoveries and technologies, came to a sudden halt. Beginning in France in the mid-19th century, a series of vineyard pests and diseases that affected the grapevines. This situation was completely new to Europeans, because other than the small, easily-managed pests encountered during Medieval and classical times, they had never experienced a problem of this type. Toward the end of the 19th century, the accustomed stability and control of the vines ended abruptly with the appearance of oidium (powdery mildew), phylloxera, and other diseases such as peronospera (downy mildew).

The continuous intercontinental contact that took place during the 19th century was responsible for the increasingly frequent presence of phytosanitary problems. In a context of global exchange and the discovery of the flora and fauna of distant and exotic lands, it is no wonder that the co-existence of vegetal species from different continents had brought about this type of problem because autochthonous species lacked sufficient defense mechanisms to confront new natural enemies. The 19th century thus marks the beginning of viticultural phytosanitary problems, which mostly emigrated from the United States toward ecosystems that were not equipped with the necessary natural defenses.

Chile is a case in point, as nearly all the pests and diseases that affect its vineyards, with the exception of *Margarodes vitis*, have been imported from neighboring countries. The most recent is downy mildew, a fungus contained in the central-south of the country and that attacks in especially rainy years. However, there are many other devastating examples that have not reached Chilean soils, such as Pierce's Disease, which has long affected North American vineyards. This bacterial disease was once transported by a single locust that was capable of flying over the perimeters of the vineyard. Today, however, a second vector, or carrier, exists in the form a particularly incisive locust called the glassy-winged sharpshooter, which reproduces easily and is capable of penetrating to the very heart of the vineyards.

Oidium

Urbanization and the expansion of parks and public spaces in mid-19th century England and France generated great interest in plants and gardens and spurred an intercontinental exchange of ornamental shrubs and fruit trees. The species brought from the Americas to Europe were one of the causes of the new diseases and insects that appeared in the Old World. Around 1846, a disease was detected in the gardens at the Château de Versailles that varied from those already known to seriously affect rosebushes in southern France. Another disease developed simultaneously in vineyards, not only in France, but in Algiers, Greece, Hungary, Italy, Spain, Switzerland, and Turkey as well. The first was studied in 1855 by a British gardener named Tucker and was classified as a new species of fungus called *Oidium tuckerii*, and later known as "powdery mildew". The second, which affected grapevines, was identified around the same time, and classified as *Uncinula necator*. This disease of North American origin arrived in Europe with the frequent commercial travel realized at the time. Its appearance on the old continent not only affected ornamental plants and shrubs, but *Vitis vinifera sativa* as well, which was discovered to be highly susceptible to its effects.

The fungus did not kill the European species, but drastically reduced its level of production. The shortage of grapes generated a major decrease in Europe's wine supply, illustrated by the drop in production from 29,000,000 hectoliters in 1840 to just 11,000,000 in 1854. Once it was discovered that sulfur could be used to combat the fungus, it was finally possible to slow and even halt the damage, although the need to apply the substance as a preventative measure after every rain or under conditions of high relative humidity meant an increase in production costs and wine prices.

Chile has achieved a rather peaceful coexistence with the fungus through basic preventative measures; fortunately, the central viticultural zone, part of the central-south and of course the north receive little or no rain in the spring, summer, and fall, favoring low environmental humidity, which in turn discourages fungal growth. One of the solutions developed in French vineyards, now used by some Chileans as well, is to plant rosebushes at the ends of the rows. Roses are susceptible to *Oidium tuckerii*, which is similar to the species that attacks grapevines, but are more sensitive under the conditions that generate it, and consequently to *Uncinula necator*. This makes rosebushes an efficient alarm system for vine growers to warn against the possible attack of the variety that affects their vines.

Phylloxera

Just a few years after Oidium's massive introduction into Europe, a homopterous insect, *Viteus vitifolii*, began to attack grapevines throughout most of the world, with the exception of certain enclaves such as Chile, and became one of the most harmful pests to vegetal species ever known. *Phylloxera vastatrix*, named by French botanist Jules-Emile Planchon in the 19th century, ruthlessly attacked the most important wine region of the world: France. Around 1869, viticulturists in southern France noticed that some of their vineyards were dying without apparent reason. Later analysis indicated the existence of an insect that appeared to be directly related to the problem. The leaves were taken to a greenhouse outside west London in 1869, where Professor Westwood of the University of Oxford identified the insect as belonging to the phylloxeride family. The bewilderment was absolute. It was several years before a remedy was discovered, and in two decades, phylloxera had extended throughout France and a large part of Europe, leaving destruction and ruin in its path. It reached Portugal and Turkey in 1871, Austria and Hungary in 1872, Switzerland in 1873, Spain in 1875, Italy in 1879, and Germany in 1881.

Phylloxera-induced lesions in the plant's root system cause weakening and eventual death. The vegetation is weakened, the leaves lose their color, and the vine cannot resist more than two or three years. In addition to phylloxera's drastic consequences on the

Phylloxera vastatrix, or simply Phylloxera, attacked France in the mid-19th century, devastating the world's most important vitivinicultural region.

This North American insect produces a series of lesions in the vines, debilitating its vegetation. The color fades from the leaves, and the plant dies in a couple years.

vine, it also reproduces quickly and easily. Its annual metamorphosis makes it a dreaded insect: in the spring it lives in the roots, then winged females appear in summer and lay their eggs in the leaves. The next generation is born and the cycle begins again. Phylloxera, which comes from North America, east of the Rocky Mountains, dramatically manifested itself in the European vineyard in the late 19th century, which was defenseless before this new enemy, and caused devastation throughout viticultural world. Few vineyards escaped its first attack: Cypress, Greece, the Canary Islands, Egypt, Australia, Argentina, Brazil, Uruguay, Chile, and specific parts of older wine regions. The other regions slowly succumbed, however, leaving Chile alone, as the only country in the world to remain completely free of the plague.

Phylloxera's previous absence in Europe is attributed to the fact that maritime connections between North America and Europe were limited to slow-moving sailing ships and that the insect died before reaching its destination. Shorter steamship voyages and more frequent travel included more plants taken to European territories, effectively eliminating the natural barrier.

Phylloxera is immune to all chemical and biological control, yet paradoxically, it was the same American vines that carried the scourge to the Old World that made it possible to combat it. In effect, grafting the European *Vitis vinifera* vines onto resistant American rootstocks made it possible for them to survive. Another practice was the genetic hybridization of American vines and *Vitis vinifera sativa*. The process produced phylloxera-resistant hybrids, also called "direct producers," which proved resistant to the insect, although these vines produce low-quality wines.

The damage produced by phylloxera was not limited to Europe however; it also generated problems in North America when vines were transported from their natural habitat between the Atlantic Coast and the Rocky Mountains and California on the Pacific Coast. Sources debate the date of the introduction – either 1858 or 1873 – and it is unknown whether it was imported from Europe or brought with the American variety *Vitis labrusca concord*, used for juice. In Australia it was detected for the first time in the early 1870s in the Victoria area, and in New South Wales in 1880. Just a few years later it was found in South America, spreading from Argentina, Brazil, and then the rest of the Americas, except Chile, which still remains free of the insect today.

Chile's privileged condition has sparked interest among entomologists and other scientists who attempt to understand the various reasons for the absence of phylloxera in the country. Some theories point to its geographic isolation; the

Atacama Desert to the north, glacial ice to the south, the Andes Mountains to the east, and the Pacific Ocean to the west. Another theory, defended by Italian Professor Mario Fregoni, sustains that Chile's natural soil, water, and environmental conditions do not allow phylloxera to survive, which detracts from the geographic barrier theory.

The most popular explanation given today is the Chilean government's astute decision to prohibit the importation of grapevines into the country upon learning of the existence of phylloxera in 1877. When the insect reached Buenos Aires in 1870, alarmed Chilean authorities erected a strict protective barrier that remains in effect today. This barrier prohibited the entrance of any soil-carrying root, organic fertilizers, shrubs or similar plant through a decree that was improved throughout the 20th century, until it finally banned any vegetal material from entering the country except under conditions of strict quarantine control. Compliance with the decree is currently controlled by the National Agricultural and Livestock Service (S.A.G.).

Phylloxera's appearance in the late 19th century in most of the world's vineyards not only damaged the grapevine and its image, but also brought negative economic consequences due to the high costs of replanting, shorter vineyard life spans, the development of viral diseases, analyses of physiological affinity that arise during grafting, and other problems that continue to the present day.

At one time Chile used its absence of phylloxera as a major selling point abroad, but this marketing strategy proved to be a double-edged sword. Not only is phylloxera a delicate subject in European circles, but should the disease eventually break out in Chile, the damage it would do to the image of national wines would be considerable. On the other hand, although it is true that Chile was very fortunate to import noble varieties before the invasion of phylloxera, it is not true that uninfected vines were re-sent to Europe to save that continent's vines, as some people have stated. Chile's status as the only major wine-producing country that can cultivate vines without grafting has meant economic advantages, and according to some, has imparted a more genuine character to Chilean wines.

Appellations of Origin

The first legal classifications for appellations of origin were created in 1935, but the first non-official signs of the system date back to 70 AD or even earlier, because wine, as any other good, needed to be classified in order to estimate its commercial value. The appellation of origin system designated the source of a specific product whose characteristics were defined in accordance to the geographical zone from which it came. When this is applied to wine, its objectives are to protect the geographic origin and determine the way in which it was made, such as the varieties used, encouraging the organization of the productive sector and facilitating its identification and trade and international markets. As English consumers related the quality of a wine with its producer, the geographical zones that produced the best quality were identified with greater precision. The interest in knowing the places that generated prestigious wines generated the concept of *terroir*, determined by the combined influence of geography, soil and climate on wine. The human element was later introduced as a new differentiating factor, giving rise to the different Crus, or vineyards that produce wines of exceptional quality and character.

France

The first official classifications were made in Bordeaux in 1855 with the objective of presenting the wines of the region in the *Exposition Universelle* of Paris. Bordeaux negociants were in charge of the classification, which included a sample of wines from all the major producers, including those that made common wines as well as the so-called *cru classe*. In the elite level of this class, the *premiers crus*, were Château Lafite-Rothschild, Château Latour, Château Margaux, and Château Haut-Brion. Château Mouton-Rothschild was later added in 1973.

THE MÉDOCS CLASSIFIED 1855

PREMIERS CRUS	COMMUNE	HECTARES	CASES
Château Lafite -Rothschild	Pauillac	70	36,000
Château Latour	Pauillac	65	36,700
Château Margaux	Margaux	78	33,300
Château Haut-Brion	Pessac-Leognan	43	16,000
Château Mouton-Rothschild*	Pauillac	75	27,500
*Château Mouton-Rothschild was added in PREMIERS CRUS in 1973			

At the time of the Paris Exhibition, the Rothschild's were just beginning to produce fine wines. In 1853, Nathaniel Rothschild, of the British side of the family, acquired a vineyard called Château Brane-Mouton in the Medoc, north of Bordeaux. Its name was changed to Château Mouton-Rothschild in 1930, adopting the emblem of the ram, related to the Mouton (sheep) and with the zodiac sign (Aries) of the heir, Philippe de Rothschild. Upon his death, his daughter Philippine de Rothschild took charge of the fine wine business. In 1868, James Rothschild, on the French side, invested in Château Lafite, also in the Medoc, This winery acquired great prestige when it earned a place in the premiers crus category, which it has maintained to the day under the management of Baron Elie de Rothschild and his successor, Eric de Rothschild. Château Mouton's original 1855 classification as a second cru was later modified due to the determination of its descendents, who convinced the National Institute of Appellations of Origin to incorporate Château Mouton among the *premiers crus*.

The *cru classe* classification included the best red and sweet white wines, but no dry white wines. In the 1855 Bordeaux classification, the red wines were ordered in five levels according to their quality: *Premiers Crus, Deuxiemes Crus, Troisiemes Crus, Quatriemes Crus*, and *Cinquiemes Crus*. The sweet whites were grouped into three levels: *Premier Grand Crus, Premiers Crus*, and *Deuxiemes Crus*. The Burgundy crus received the names of *climats* (a synonym of cru) *domaine, clos, or finage*.

The proposed classification for French wines was followed in part by other European countries, such as Spain, Italy, and Germany, who adapted the system to their own circumstances, according to the procedures that agree with

James Rothschild acquired Château Lafite in Medoc (Bordeaux) in 1868. The winery reached great prestige in the 1855 premier cru category; where it remains to this day.

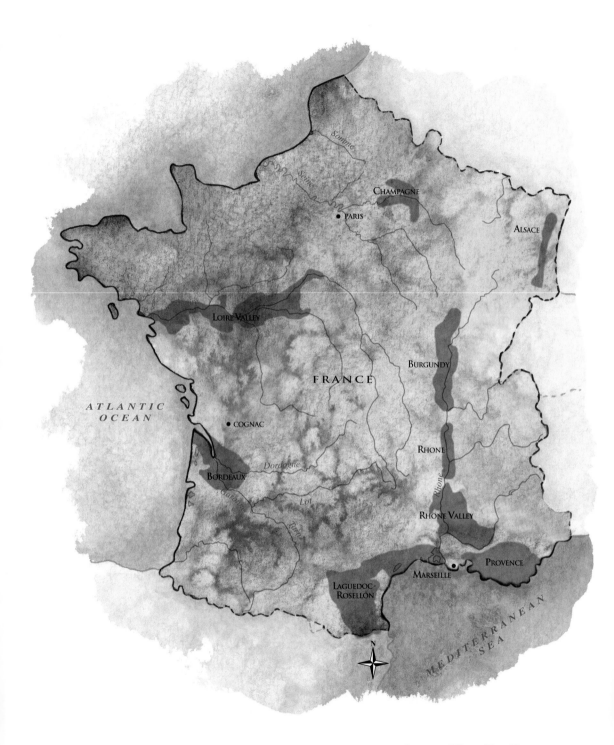

ATLANTIC
OCEAN

FRANCE

Somme

Source

CHAMPAGNE

PARIS

ALSACE

LOIRE VALLEY

BURGUNDY

COGNAC

RHONE

Dordogne

BORDEAUX

Lot

Tarn

RHONE VALLEY

PROVENCE

MARSEILLE

LAGUEDOC-
ROSELLÓN

MEDITERRANEAN
SEA

N

the internal commercial needs of each country and with the structure of their respective wine industries.

Although some have criticized the French classification system, in practice, it has proved adequate. The criticism has been directed toward the standardization to which the vineyards are subjected, particularly in specific aspects such as variety, management of productivity, harvest dates, vinification methods, length of ageing, and other technical procedures. Wineries must obey decrees imposed by a group of specialists, impeding innovation and creativity on the part of the individual vineyards and winemakers. The system of classification of denomination of origin influenced the creation of legislation to control and regulate the winemaking process, from the most prestigious to the most humble.

Current French legislation requires:

- *Vin de Table* (Table Wines) must contain at least 8.5% alcohol.

- *Vin de Pays* (Regional Wine) the elite of the *Vin de Table*, must comply with specific standards of quality, use the recommended varieties, come from a specific territory, contain a natural minimum of 10% alcohol, and maintain analytical characteristics defined by tasting committees.

- *VQDS Vin Délimite de Qualité Supérieure* or Delimited Wine of Superior Quality, wine in this category are regulated by the INAO, *Institut Nacional des Appellations d'Origine* (National Institute of Appellations of Origin)

- *AOC Appellations d'Origine Contrôlée* or Controlled Appellation of Origin, must adhere to the strict conditions specified by the INAO: area of production, grape varieties, minimum alcohol strength, maximum yield, and viticultural practices for growing and pruning, vinification, and in some cases even ageing conditions. All French wines that aspire to an *AOC* title must submit to an analytical examination and tasting. This is followed by a series of control tastings and very strict standards that the French employ to *"guarantee that the continuous quality of the products with an appellation of origim."*

Spain

After France and Italy, Spain has one of Europe's largest surface areas planted to vine. Its tradition and relationship with wine dates back to the commercial contacts established with the Phoenicians and the expansion of the Roman Empire. One of the first Denominations of Origin (Demarcation of Region) on the Iberian Peninsula was founded by Portugal's *Companhia Geral da agricultura das Vinhas do Alto Duoro.*

Spain later began to implement a system that subdivided the product between quality wines and table wines and differentiate between the wines that carried the *Denominación de Origen* (DO) from those that did not. The concept was officially defined by law in 1936, allowing for the production of wine by small proprietors to gain prestige. Quality wines are identified as VCPRD or Quality Wine Produced in Determined Region, and must be selected by the *Consejo Regulador* (Regulatory body) of each region.

Toward the end of the 19th century, Spanish vitiviniculture entered a new stage of modernization. The Torres family, who have led the process of modernizing the Catalonian wine industry, founded their winery in Vilafranca de Penedes in 1870.

The classification prior to becoming a DO is the *Vino de la Tierra* (Regional Wine) denomination. This group is part of the Table Wine categories, but is distinguished by having higher than average quality and coming from an area with its own specific character.

The Spanish system grants the *Denominación de Origen Calificada* (DOCa) to the DOs whose products have clear affinities with their place of origin, for example, the wines of La Rioja.

One of Spain's most prestigious wineries is that of the Torres family in Vilafranca de Penedes, founded in 1870. This winery was largely responsible for initiating Spain's process of modernizing winemaking in Catalonia.

THE CONTEMPORARY ERA
IN THE NEW WORLD
The beginning of Prestige Wines

The search to produce fine wines incorporated the use of new technologies, such as a portable rail system called the decauville that allowed grapes to be quickly transported from the vineyard to the winery without damaging the roots of the plants they way the thin wheels of the carts did. View looking from Viña Cousiño Macul toward Santiago in 1880.

The renovation of vitivinicultural technologies in Europe marked the beginning of a new development in the wine industry that resulted in increased production and remarkable improvements in wine quality. The New World was able to participate in this development due to the arrival of new techniques and knowledge that allowed improvements in production, legislation, and the establishment of economic policies to foster the industry. However, those processes had different rhythms and results in the different countries.

CHILE

By 1800, the land that Spanish Conquistador Pedro de Valdivia described in his letters to King Charles V in 1541 as the best and most fertile in the world was inhabited by a mestizo population of nearly 700,000 people. This eminently rural population was concentrated in the Central Valley between the Aconcagua and Maipo Rivers, practiced subsistence farming, and had small-scale industries in chicha, wine, and aguardiente, as well as merchandize imported from Peru and occasionally from Europe. During the early decades of the 19th century, Latin American colonies began to exercise political emancipation, which began in Chile with the creation of its first governing body in 1810. This new context allowed an international opening that would be expressed with the arrival of travelers, intellectuals, and investors over the course of the coming decades.

The arrival of foreign immigrants, especially from France, who knew how to reform and renovate the haciendas was key to agricultural development. Many of those immigrants amassed great fortunes and joined the established aristocracy, strengthening the *latifundio*, which continued to symbolize prestige and power. In the mid-19th century, Chile's accelerated economic development from silver, copper, and later nitrate mining generated a degree of prosperity beyond previous imagination that allowed investment in the infrastructure that modified rural spaces in general and the Central Valley in particular. The ports began to receive steam ships, railroads extended throughout the territory, the telegraph provided

The Chilean wines of the mid-19th century did not meet the standards of the refined aristocratic palate, one of the reasons behind the importation of new varieties, oak casks, and vinification techniques from France.

CHILEAN WINE. THE HERITAGE

links between distant towns and cities, and property-owners began to improve their lands, which influenced the later increase in agricultural production.

The knowledge acquired by the Chilean aristocracy in its European travels was expressed upon their return in the incorporation of new trends and changes in lifestyle, particularly with respect to gastronomy. The previously existing wines were made from rustic varieties brought by the Conquistadors, primarily the red variety País or the white Moscatel de Alejandría (also called Italia). These local wines lost favor with the increasingly refined aristocratic palate, which encouraged national production of fine wines, similar to those they had consumed in Spain and France.

This new spirit introduced many new French and German varieties to Chile, including the red varieties Cabernet Franc, Cabernet Sauvignon, Cot or Malbec, Merlot, Verdot, and Carmenère, as well as Sauvignon Blanc, Chardonnay, Semillon, Riesling, and Gewürztraminer in whites. If the adaptation of the first vines brought by the Conquistadors was good, that of the selected European varieties was even better, as not only did they reproduce the positive characteristics, but they were also carefully selected and cultivated. History tells us that Silvestre Ochagavía was the first to introduce these varieties in 1851, but historian José del Pozo has shown that it was probably Nourrichet who introduced these vines in 1845, or even Claudio Gay fifteen years earlier.

The new vines began to replace the old colonial varieties, which included not only those mentioned above, but *Aceituna*, *Cristalina Blanca*, *Huasquina*, and *Moscatel Rosada*. These varieties produced mediocre wines under rather precarious conditions. For example, grapes were dried to make so-called generous (fortified) wines, from Cauquenes to Concepción. The *asoleado*, or sun-baked, wine made in Cauquenes was very popular in Chile until quite recently. Among the poor and country people, there is still a large interest in a style of wine called *pipeño*, which is simply poorly vinified, unfiltered and often homemade wine that has been shown to be quite dangerous to health.

Claudio Gay's writings indicate that in the mid-19th century, there were approximately 30,000 hectares of viniferous vines in Chile, distributed primarily in Concepción (15,500 ha), the Aconcagua Valley (5,000 ha), Cauquenes (4,500 ha), Santiago (2,000 ha), Coquimbo (1,600 ha), Colchagua (1,240 ha), and Talca (700 ha). Vitiviniculture in those times extended from south to north, due to the development of dry-farmed agriculture and the increase of the irrigation systems of the central area. The irrigated surface rose to 440,000 hectares in 1875, and was nearly double that in 1900, thanks to the initiative of the agriculturalists who extended the existing systems and built dams and canals. Along with the increase of irrigated lands, the incorporation of territory south of the Bío Bío and the conquest of nitrate regions after the Pacific War contributed to expansion and helped open new internal markets, allowing the increase of the national wine trade.

Vineyards made up a large part of the cultivated lands. Given that the population of 1850 is estimated to be 1,400,000 people, it is possible to say that the vitivinicultural activity was proportionally more important then than it is today. The density was 50 people per hectare of planted vine in 1850, while today it is 146 people per hectare.

Viña Santa Carolina was founded in 1875 by Luis Pereira-Cotapos. His brick and stone winery mortared with lime and egg white was named a National Monument in 1973.

CHILEAN WINE. THE HERITAGE

The Beginning of Prestige Wineries

Although it can be said that vitiviniculture was one of the most prosperous 19th-century agricultural activities, as is indicated by the increase in production, of the 51,000,000 liters produced in 1875 to 110,000,000 liters in 1884, the primary benefit of owning a winery was the prestige it carried, especially when it bore the name of the owners. A similar trend was taking place in France, where were wineries bought up by wealthy bankers and merchants, such as the Rothschild family, who acquired Château Mouton in 1853 and Château Lafite in 1868. The competition generated between them required the introduction of improvements in the quality of its red wines and it is interesting to observe that the majority of the old wineries still exist today, although few continue in the hands of their founding families.

The major Chilean wineries that emerged during the second half of the 19th century included: Silvestre Ochagavía's Viña Ochagavía, whose main facilities were located in the Subercaseaux plain; José Tomás Urmeneta's Viña Urmeneta, located in San Francisco de Limache; and that of Maximiano Errázuriz and his son Rafael Errázuriz, known as Viña Errázuriz Panquehue, located in the province now known as San Felipe. The Viña Conchalí in North Santiago belonged to José Joaquín Aguirre; Viña San Pedro in Lontue to Bonifacio Correa-Albano; Viña Cousiño Macul in Peñalolén belonged to Luis Cousiño; Viña Lontue in Lontue was founded by Francisco Correa-Errázuriz; Viña Santa Rita in Alto Jahuel belonged to Domingo Fernández-Concha; Viña Carmen, in Buin to Cristián Lanz; Viña Santa Carolina in Macul to Luis Pereira; Viña Concha y Toro in Pirque to Melchor Concha y Toro; and Viña Santa Ana in Talagante to Francisco Undurraga.

These vineyards launched the first features of 20th century vitiviniculture, which transformed the industry from an artisanal endeavor that sold bulk wines through commercial agents to one that sold its bottled wines directly, both in Chile and abroad. The beginning of Chile's wine companies is related to the early fortunes produced through the exploitation of nitrate, coal mines, and agriculture, among them Melchor Concha y Toro, Luis Cousiño, Maximiano Errázuriz, Domingo Fernández-Concha, and Francisco Undurraga. This group of outstanding businessmen founded major wineries that are still completely active today in the early 21st century.

Concha y Toro Winery

Melchor Concha y Toro was born in 1833, the son of Melchor de Santiago Concha y Cerda and Damiana Toro. He married Emiliana Subercaseaux y Vicuña. He was an attorney and congressman in Melipilla, Santiago, and Chillán and was elected to preside over the House of Representatives in 1876. He was the Minister of Finance during the presidency of José Joaquín Pérez, Senator for Ñuble and Santiago, and was known for encouraging commerce with Argentina. He excelled in business as the president of the Huanchaca Mining Company in Bolivia. As devout Roman Catholics and philanthropists, he and his wife Emiliana founded the Children's Protection Society.

He created the Concha y Toro Winery in 1883, deciding to take advantage of the vitivinicultural potential of the Maipo Valley. The company originated in Pirque on land inherited by his wife.

In 1875, Melchor Concha y Toro put his wife in charge of the construction of the hacienda house, today known as the Casona de Pirque. A few years later, don Melchor imported French vines directly from Bordeaux, which he had planted on lands bordering the Maipo River. He hired the renowned French winemaker Monsieur Labouchere, who was charged with making the winery's first wines. As a winery owner, he was dedicated to other agricultural activities through the National Agricultural Society and was one of its most resolute collaborators. Around 1929, the Concha y Toro Winery had 95 hectares of vineyards in addition to the 143 hectares planted on lands belonging to Emiliana Subercaseaux in Cachapoal.

The Concha y Toro manor house and its surrounding park in Pirque were built in 1875 by Melchor Concha y Toro and reflect the French spirit in architecture and landscaping that the 19th-century winery owners sought after.

120

Cousiño Macul Winery

The foundations for the Cousiño Macul Winery were laid by Luis Cousiño-Squella, who died before his buildings were completed. His widow, Isidora Goyenechea, inaugurated the facility in 1878 and hired the renowned French winemaker Pierre Godefroy Durand. Don Luis Cousiño was the only child of the businessman and mining magnate Matías Cousiño and his first wife Loreto Squella. In 1841 his father was remarried to Luz Gallo, a wealthy widow from the north, who brought to her marriage a daughter named Isidora Goyenechea, who later married Luis and became the driving force behind the Cousiño Macul Winery.

Luis was educated in the National Institute and later traveled throughout Europe, where he learned modern techniques that he put into practice in the family coal mines his father had established in Lota and Coronel. In commercial endeavors, he promoted the silk industry, was one of Chile's pioneers of reforestation, and introduced salmon breeding in the Valdivia River. He was an outstanding politician as a liberal congressman for Lautaro and later for Santiago. An art-lover, he beautified the park in Lota, and by government request, ordered the design of Parque Cousiño in Santiago, now known as Parque O'Higgins. He built a palace on Dieciocho Avenue in Santiago, where the family hosted major social events. In 1872 he was transferred to Lima, Peru, where he died on May 19, 1873. Upon the death of his wife Isidora, the Cousiño Macul Winery passed to the hands of their son, Arturo Cousiño and later to grandson, Arturo Cousiño-Lyon, who together established the foundations for making high-quality prestige wines.

Viña Cousiño Macul was one of the first to incorporate the decauville system of mining carts modified for use in vineyards and wineries.

Errázuriz Panquehue Winery

Don Maximiano Errázuriz was born in Santiago in 1832, the son of a Basque family that arrived in Chile in 1753. In more than two centuries of history, members of this family have been tied to major historical events and important cultural, social, and political changes.

Don Maximiano studied in Santiago and later moved to Valparaíso, one of the major ports of the time. In those years he met his future wife, Amalia Urmeneta, daughter of José Tomás Urmeneta, one of the wealthiest men in Chile. He and his father-in-law formed a copper refining company, and in 1856 he created the Santiago Gas Company, which was responsible for the capital's public lighting. The couple moved to the north to live in Guayacán, where Maximiano managed the mining business. After the death of his wife, he left his children under the care of his mother and moved north of Valparaíso so he could be closer to them.

Maximiano Errázuriz began planting vines in Panquehue in 1870. True to his pioneering spirit, he incorporated modern technology in his vineyards and winery in order to make wine in the Aconcagua Valley.

Don Maximiano was an active participant in Chile's public life. He occupied a seat in the House of Representatives for the first time at age 25 and was later elected Senator of the Republic for 9 years. In 1870, following the example of his father-in-law, he decided to plant vineyards in Panquehue in the Aconcagua Valley, north of Santiago. As opposed to other families that established wineries close to Santiago, and following his pioneering spirit, he chose a site that was farther from the capital. When he planted his vineyards he commented:

> *"Grapevines should be carefully tended and treated like a work of art, since their life span runs parallel to that of humans. A vine should be educated, cared for, and trained like a man; it should not be allowed to grow unoriented, because to bear proper fruits, it must not extend its branches in vain."*

He met Carmen Valdés, daughter of the Governor of Valparaíso, in 1871. They married and he began construction on a great house in Panquehue. His wife contracted yellow fever during a trip abroad and died. Maximiano decided to build a new house in Santiago, which is today the seat of the Brazilian Embassy. His children were all married by 1883, and he returned definitively to Panquehue and his vineyards, where he had planted 300 hectares of vines. He died in 1890, at 58 years of age. His son Rafael Errázuriz later increased the vineyards to 700 hectares.

Santa Rita Winery

Domingo Fernández-Concha, son of Pedro Fernández and Rosa de Santiago Concha de la Cerda, was born in Santiago on April 15, 1838. He was a distinguished businessman and founded the Domingo Fernández Concha Bank. He belonged to the Conservative Party and formed the Catholic Youth Circle with Abdón Cifuentes in late 1876. He was elected Senator of Chiloé in 1894 to replace the deceased Vicente Sanfuentes-Fernández. He was later elected Senator for Maule.

In 1880, Domingo Fernández-Concha founded the Santa Rita Winery on his *hacienda* in Buin. He planted vineyards according to a modern model of agricultural and industrial exploitation and hired winemaker Fernando Saligne to manage them. The *hacienda* had clean and comfortable rooms for the workers, as well as a school, chapel, the San Rafael Entertainment Circle, a theater, and continuous social assistance. The large park was meticulously cared for so that the students of Santiago's Catholic schools and neighboring students could rest under the cedars, wellingtonias (*sequoias*), and chestnuts.

The large neo-gothic manor house at Viña Santa Rita, founded by Domingo Fernández-Concha, displays the splendor that surrounded the great vintners of the late 19th century.

Domingo Fernández-Concha died on November 2, 1919 at the age of 73. Following his death, the company was owned by the García-Huidobro family until the 1970s. The Spanish Crown had awarded Vicente García-Huidobro, father of the well-known Chilean poet Vicente Huidobro, the noble title of *Marqués de Casa Real,* which inspired the name of one of the winery's most important wines.

The winery building is of particular interest. Erected in 1875 by French architects, it has since been declared a National Monument for its history and type of construction, which includes arched vaults made with a mortar of *cal y canto*: egg white, sand, and limestone, to cement the bricks together.

Undurraga Winery

In 1882, Francisco Undurraga, owner of a fortune that originated in agriculture rather than silver or nitrate mining, bought a property called San Vicente de Talagante in the Maipo Valley in a public auction. The estate was later renamed Santa Ana in honor of his wife Ana Fernández. He brought the first vines from France and Germany that same year and planted an extension of 30 blocks. He installed irrigation systems with the expertise of agricultural engineer M. Pressac. From France he brought Cabernet Sauvignon, Sauvignon Blanc, Merlot, and Pinot Noir, and from Germany, Riesling and Gewürztraminer from Bonn, Coblenza, Cologne, and Frankfurt. With a perfectionist's spirit he guided the construction of the winery's park designed by French landscape architect Pierre Dubois, as well as the construction of the winery facilities in 1890. He paid special attention to the fabrication of containers and the use of oak from Kentucky and Bosnia.

Francisco Undurraga was one of Chile's viticultural pioneers. In 1884 he planted French varieties such as Cabernet Sauvignon, Sauvignon Blanc, Merlot, and Pinot Noir, along with German varieties such as Riesling and Gewürztraminer at his Santa Ana estate.

Winery Development

In order to revive old wineries and bring new ones to life, Chilean investors turned to foreign technicians, particularly French specialists in vine management, vinification, and the conservation of finished wines. Among the outstanding winemakers of the early years were Joseph Bertrand, who came to work in Viña Ochagavía; Germán Bachelet, in Viña Santa Carolina; Martín Percheux, in Viña Subercaseaux, and Alfredo Gabarroche, in Viña Urmeneta. These winemakers were not only concerned with the progress of the technique, but with the design and aesthetics of the winery itself. The owners therefore invited renowned French architects to Chile to direct the construction of their facilities. The edification of underground cellars followed French trends and represented the presence of modern construction concepts. Modern viticultural and enological machinery and equipment were also imported at that time, along with noble woods used to construct on site the foudres and tanks that were used for the next 100 years.

In the vineyards, grapes were transported using the newly-adopted *decauville,* a type of small train that could be disassembled and repositioned as the harvest progressed, thereby eliminating the need for heavy ox-carts to enter between the rows, which damaged the development of the vines root systems. It is quite likely that the use of the *decauville* was an adaptation of a system used in the mines at that time since the majority of winery owners also had investment in the mining industry. In the commercial area, Chilean wines began to be exported to Europe in 1887. Macario Ossa (*Viña La Rosa*) is credited with the

Winery owners brought foreign technicians, especially French specialists, to Chile.

CHILEAN WINE. THE HERITAGE

first registered sale. Chronicles indicate that Ossa was encouraged by the success of Chilean wines in the Vienna Exposition in 1873. Guillermo Brown is another renowned exporter, and there are records of Chile's successful participation in European wine fairs in Bordeaux 1882, Liverpool 1885, and Paris in 1889. By the early 20th century, the wine industry of the Central Zone had successfully developed, the selected European varieties were established, and the wineries were supervised and managed by French technicians.

The Undurraga Winery sent its first exports to the United States in 1903. In 1910, Chilean President Pedro Montt took 200 cases of wine to Argentina to celebrate the country's centennial. The Santa Ana Rhin wine was so well received that it won the Argentine National Shield Award. The emblem was later proudly displayed on the wine label.

On the other hand, the rise of Chilean educational centers promoted the training of professionals who would later replace the need for foreign technicians. Manuel Rojas, an agricultural engineer, was a product of this training. He was sent to Europe by the Chilean government in 1900 to travel through France, Spain, Portugal, and Italy. He wrote the major work *Viticultura y Vinificación* (Viticulture and Vinification), in which he related the changes and processes underway in Chilean vineyards and wines.

> *"It is gratifying for the love of one's own nation to see that we are not inferior to France or other countries in matters of vineyard care and vinification. Our landowners are vitally concerned with and interested in good vineyard and winery management and have become competent through observation and by reading special treatises. Because their routines are not firmly established, they can easily assimilate advances that arrive from the Old World and acquire better material for their work, leaving aside that which is already outdated."*

Manuel Rojas describes in detail the experimental use of cold temperatures in vinifications conducted by winemaker Vicente Valdivia-Urbina in 1924, as developed by the Department of Viticulture and Enology of the Ministry of Agriculture, indicating that *"One of the most interesting applications of cold is in vinifying white wines at low temperatures."* Those first attempts made in the 1920s only began to become widespread during the 1980s. In the same text, the author also manifests a number of criticisms regarding the way in which the wine industry had developed, primarily with respect to the contrast between the brilliant *"progress of viticulture and the regrettable management of vinification."* He also expressed serious complaints about the lack of sanitation observed in handling the containers and the lack of appropriate machinery in the wineries.

It is interesting to note that this refers to the wineries located primarily in the central irrigated zone, between Santiago and Curicó, where the production of fine wines began. However, the majority of the production originated in varieties such as País and Moscatel de Alejandría, generating common wines of questionable quality and which were often adulterated in the taverns and commercial establishments. This reflection has not been duly considered by analysts of the subject, despite its importance, as most of the winegrowers and the vineyards were in this situation, which is visible even today among the small growers in certain areas of the 8th and 9th regions.

The consequences of vitivinicultural development were not only felt in rural areas, but in the cities that were home to the owners of great fortunes as well. The industry's political and economic scenario in the early 20th century is reflected in the texts derived from the *First National Wine Congress,* held in Santiago in early January 1933 and published by the National Vitivinicultural Union. During this congress, the first complaints were heard against the crises of overproduction generated in a nation where the average wine consumption reached 90 liters per person per year in the 1930s. The account by conservative political leader Tomás Cox reports successive crises of overproduction that took place between 1909 and 1931. Also worthy of note is the fact that Cox was correct in expressing his skepticism regarding Chile's possibilities as a wine exporting country; despite the recent repeal of North American dry laws he said, *"Export, yes, but it is not a solution for any global aspect, given the low volumes produced."* It took nearly sixty years to prove him wrong.

Chile's Négociants

The mid-19th century modernization of the wine industry brought with it increased sales. *The Vicuña Mackenna Catalonians,* a distinguished group of Spaniards who arrived in Chile in the early 20th century played an important role in this process. Nearly all of their wineries were strategically located on Vicuña Mackenna Avenue, which was in direct contact with the network of southern railroads via the rail connection in the old San Eugenio Station. They were known for managing wine market sales; they bought wine from producers and resold it to retailers, taverns, canteens, and shops, where it was purchased by consumers. They bought wine from medium and large bulk wine producers and prepared it for resale in 15-liter *chuicos*, 10-liter demijohns, or 5-liter jugs that were delivered to bars and restaurants and sold door-to-door, based on cash sales plus the return or exchange of empty containers.

Deliveries were made in 5-ton trucks with a carriage that only covered the central portion and rode low, close to the axles, so that containers could be handled with a minimum of lifting. The empty containers were placed over the center portion of the body.

These merchants, or "industrialists" as they called themselves, were extraordinarily reliable, trustworthy, and honest in their business dealings and payments. Proof of this was the value of the "Catalonian promissory note." The group's solid financial solvency allowed them to pay in installments, usually with one payment for every thousand arrobas (40,000 liters), the first due at 90 days. Winegrowers in need of financing could sell their crops en *primieur* prior to the future harvest. Those involved clearly understood that the deal was based on the reputation of their signature and that if they failed to comply with their commitments, they would no longer be considered clients. The transaction was therefore valid from both the commercial perspective and the strategies used for suitable and timely purchasing and financing.

The wine itself was generally quite mediocre, but by handling the raw material correctly, it certainly complied with the objective of supplying beverages for quick consumption at appropriate prices for customers who were not very demanding. In general, the technical management of the wineries was an example of neither hygiene nor modernity, as they only performed very basic operations: blending, clarifying, and filtering, in accordance with the needs of the market.

The marketing and sales of bulk wines facilitated watering the product, falsification, and in some cases even use of saccharine as a sweetening agent, which was one of the most common infractions. These violations should have been detected by controls performed by the Internal Revenue Department, which regulated the industry until 1979, when the responsibility passed to the Agriculture and Livestock Service (SAG).

The problem of adulterated wines was accentuated in more remote areas, such as in the nitrate mines, where the great demand for alcohol and infrequent inspections led commercial agents to continually protect and defend the validity of their products, publishing warnings in newspapers about adulterations and the incorrect use of brand names.

The relationship between these businessmen and Chilean viticulturists, the vast majority of whom were members of the most traditional rural aristocracy, was complex and difficult. This promoted the development of the called "wine brokers", who had the special ability of facilitating commercial contact between buyers and sellers, usually without ever meeting personally. These brokers, dressed in camelhair coats and banded hats, with the perennial cigar in their mouths, driving long-tailed automobiles (in the worst of cases a Chevy Impala), and with enough time to chat about everything under the sun for hours on end, were known for being gentlemen with great common sense and clearly endowed with a sharp sense of psychological perception, capable of charming both the hard-working Catalonian businessman and the *hacienda* owner with lordly airs.

The Vicuña Mackenna negociants handled local wine distribution. They bought the wine for resale to vendors, taverns, canteens, and shops.

The brokers not only made the contacts and helped the parties reach an agreement, but also wrote the contracts, deposited the bank notes issued by the buyers, and very often even cashed the checks and deposited the money in the sellers' checking accounts.

Within this commercial design, the difficulties of interpretation of the contracts never ended up in the courts of law, as the parties themselves established an independent arbitrator to resolve any contingency, a role that fell to attorney Francisco Pérez-Errázuriz, whose rulings were never questioned. The prosperous activity of this commercial group, such as other agents and merchants, began to decline in the late 1960s, for various reasons. The first was the beginning of an active competition between traditional wineries, led by Concha y Toro, San Pedro, Santa Rita, and Santa Carolina, who had been quite withdrawn from vitivinicultural activity since the 1930s. Furthermore, the wineries themselves began to participate more in sales and distribution. A third significant factor took place in 1964 when the production tax paid by wine producers was replaced by the Purchase and Sales Tax, that the wineries were required to charge and retain, which had a significant financial impact.

Another factor that affected the business of the merchants was the decrease in national and international wine consumption, which was replaced by beer, pisco, soft drinks, ice cream, and types of recreation that limited conversation, favoring visual and more dynamic types of entertainment.

The result was that the Catalonians gradually and inexorably disappeared from the Chilean commercial market, and those who had the sufficient economic backing moved on to other productive and business activities. Miguel Viu-Manent deserves individual mention in that not only was he the last to leave the traditional market, but he also had the great vision to acquire fine wine vineyards in the province of Colchagua, where he created the Viu Manent Winery, which now produces prestigious, high-quality wines.

Taxes: the Industry Stagnates

The production of alcoholic beverages has always been a lucrative activity and has attracted the attention of authorities as a source of tax revenue since ancient times. The perception of this beverage as a dispensable luxury product and a generator of social ills has provided the justification for the application of discriminatory taxes.

During Chile's colonial period, a series of restrictions was passed that tended to favor Spanish coffers and commerce. However, taxation was not formally defined until 1902, with the creation of Law N° 1515. This gave rise to the "Alcohol Tax Administration", which became the "General Tax Directorate" in 1912, followed by the General Internal Revenue Directorate in 1916. The latter transformation established different values of annual payment per hectare in consideration of the geographic location of the vineyards. Those to the north of the Maule River paid 30 pesos per irrigated hectare and 15 pesos per non-irrigated hectare. South of the river, payment was 20 and 10 pesos respectively.

A new alcohol law passed in 1939 prohibited planting new vineyards or transplanting existing vines to more productive lands. The regulation was based on the irritation that overproduction provoked in the winery owners associated with the National Vitivinicultural Union. Added to this was the argument that alcoholism devastated the working class and reduced national production. The high per capita wine consumption reached 90 liters per year. In the international context, moralist leagues were formed to combat excessive alcohol consumption. In the United States, the dry law, or Prohibition, was promulgated in 1920.

Chilean winemakers, many of whom were important parliamentarians and in favor of limiting overproduction, found contradictory and unexpected support in the politicians of the left who considered the winery owners to be 'poisoning the people.' Therefore, when the suggestion of prohibiting the plantation of new vineyards reached parliament, it was received with unanimity.

The restrictive law was passed in 1939, voted in by the parliamentarians of the right, including Poklepovic, Errázuriz, Walker, Irarrázaval, Dussaillant (who owned the Casablanca Winery), Alessandri, Guarello, and national socialist González von Marées. The parliamentarians of the left who rejected the initiative included Faivovich, Chamudes, and Latcham. Future president Salvador Allende abstained. The left's interest in controlling and even extinguishing the wine industry was so strong that parliamentarian Aníbal Jara presented a motion to order all vineyards in national territory be torn out. Within this unique context, the law had a negative impact on medium and small producers. In general terms, the problem of over-production was controlled, and the planted surface area decreased from 106,000 to 92,000 hectares.

The law exempted those who pulled out at least part of their vineyards, which had a negative influence on the structure of national vitiviniculture, primarily on fine wine producers.

A growing change was noted at that time in favor of techniques that tended to increase productivity at the expense of quality. Around 1960, a large part of the irrigated vineyards, initially planted according to Bordeaux tradition (low-trained vines and high-density plantations) had been replaced by low density plantations using high vertical shoot positioning and even pergola training systems similar to those used for producing table grapes.

In this sense we could say that national production had 'Argentinized,' responding to demand with a very high unitary productivity which, in many cases, surpassed 30,000 liters per hectare.

This therefore gave rise to herbaceous flavors and an abrupt decrease in the traditional deep color of Chilean red wines. These actions, in addition to a series of other restraints, completely disfigured the quality of Chile's wines, although paradoxically, they did not manage to control either the supply or alcoholism, except during a very short period.

ARGENTINA

During the colonial period, Argentine vitiviniculture developed slowly and carefully due to the difficulty of overland travel to the port city and the Atlantic coast. The wine industry's explosive growth began in the 19th century due to the arrival of noble varieties in Mendoza in 1850 and the inauguration of the railroad between Buenos Aires and Mendoza in 1885, which joined the future production center with the principal consumer center. Miguel Pouget brought vines from Chile and later from France to the Quinta Normal in Mendoza. The commercialization of the wines was realized by Italian and Spanish immigrants, including Felipe Rutini, Antonio Tomba, Augusto Rafaeli, Pedro Brandi, Luis Tirasso, Pascual Toso, and Juan Giol.

Tiburcio Benegas deserves special mention. Born in Santa Fe in 1844, he moved to Mendoza in 1865, where he bought 250 hectares in Godoy Cruz and installed his El Trapiche winery. Benegas, an ambitious man with broad interests, encouraged immigration to increase qualified labor, planted French varieties from Chile and Europe, and imported advanced technologies. His exemplary work represented the efforts and difficulties faced by the businessmen of the time, reflected in a passage in the book *"La Familia Benegas y el Vino Argentino"* (The Benegas Family and Argentine Wine), written by Fernando Vidal-Buzzi.

> *"Following the advice of his father-in-law, Eusebio Blanco, Tiburcio Benegas traveled by mule to Chile in 1884 along with Emilio Civit to see the progress in trans-Andean vitiviniculture and decided to import 'French' varieties into Mendoza. Their return to Argentina was a little more complicated because snow closed the mountain pass and they had to endure the long sea voyage through the Strait of Magellan."*

Pedro Arata was another distinguished man in Argentine vitiviniculture. His work was oriented toward improving the quality of wine, which began to take place around 1920. The active competition generated by wine imported from Europe spurred an interest in imitating European techniques and qualities, which led to research trips to learn about the winemaking process.

After the Second World War, Argentina began a period of economic growth and prosperity that aided the redistribution of wealth in favor of salaried workers and generated a process of rural-to-urban migration. This generated an explosive increase in wine consumption, which resulted in governmental authorization to water the wine in an attempt to increase marketable volumes. The high demand for wine generated a spectacular increase in winery profits, resulting in new investments in wineries and vineyards oriented toward making large volumes of common wines.

In a 1998 conference entitled *Argentine Vitiviniculture: Evolution and Perspectives*, Félix R. Aguinaga described the process that gave rise to Argentina's tremendous agro-industry. One of the first indices was the slow replacement of noble varieties with other high-yield varieties destined for the production of common wines and the replacement of the vertically-positioned training systems with pergolas, which allowed for triple the production to the detriment of quality.

During this period, the wineries used nationally-produced equipment, known for its inferior technology and high prices. Devices for extracting subterranean water were employed to reduce water limitations, increase the cultivable surface area, and implement improvements in rural areas.

In the following decades the enormous development of the Argentine wine industry, supported by the high levels of internal consumption, made it the world's fifth largest wine producer. This system reached its peak in the 1970s, when the per capita consumption reached 92 liters for a population of 23 million people.

The surface area planted to vine increased by 40% between 1961 and 1977, reaching a historical maximum of 350,680 hectares. The following years brought a crisis of over-production that resulted in large-scale reductions in vineyards and consumption, accompanied by the corresponding decrease in production. At this point the industry began to stagnate, despite a small group of producers dedicated to exclusively producing quality wines. Current production hovers around 200,000 hectares.

For many years Argentine vitiviniculture focused on volume and high unitary production in its vineyards. Today, however, many of the country's producers have incorporated the objectives of nobility and quality, a goal that they are fully capable of reaching.

PERU

ICA

• LA PAZ

BOLIVIA

TARIJA

PARAGUAY

BRAZIL

TUCUMAN

LA RIOJA

SAN JUAN

RÍO GRANDE

• PORTO ALEGRE

LIMARI

URUGUAY

ACONCAGUA
CASABLANCA
MAIPO
CACHAPOAL
COLCHAGUA
MAULE
ITATA
BIOBIO

MALLECO

MENDOZA

• SANTIAGO

LA RIVERA

BUENOS AIRES •

• MONTEVIDEO

CHILE

ARGENTINA

RÍONEGRO

PACIFIC
OCEAN

CHILE

ATLANTIC
OCEAN

N

CHILEAN WINE. THE HERITAGE

BRAZIL

Due to continuous failed attempts at growing *Vitis Sativa*, Brazilian winegrowers turned to *Vitis americanas* or hybrid varieties, particularly Isabella, which Thomas Messiter planted on Marineros Island and along the banks of Río Grande do Sul in 1840. The later arrival of European immigrants to different regions of Brazil encouraged vitivinicultural production. For example, Italians arrived in Río Grande do Sul in 1875 and Germans around 1884; a new wave of Portuguese immigration began in 1860 in Santa Santarina, and French winegrowers settled in Curitiba around 1865. The influence of the immigrants led to the production of small quantities of wine from the Italian varieties Barbera, Bonarda, Moscato, Trebiano, along with a few French varieties such as Cabernet Sauvignon and Merlot, as well as the German Riesling. Some decades later in 1970, the interest for making quality wines led to foreign investment and the development of a wine industry in the southern areas, particularly in the state of Río Grande, which now has the largest surface area planted to vine and where most of Brazil's wines are produced. Predominant varieties include Pinot Noir and Merlot in reds and Chardonnay and Gewürztraminer in whites, primarily for sparkling wines, which are made in modern wineries and with modern processes to ensure quality and excellence. Brazil now has 65,000 hectares planted to vine and produces more than 3.5 million hectoliters per year. Its average wine consumption is 2 liters per year per person.

URUGUAY

Urugay's history of vineyards and winemaking began with the institution of the republic. Little information on colonial winemaking is available, except for José Manuel Catellano's work *Observaciones sobre Agricultura* (Observations on Agriculture), which claims that significant plantations of vines for the early consumption of different types of muscatels were planted in 1730. However, during the 19th century, Uruguay developed an increase in its viticultural activity with respect to the introduction of Italian varieties such as Barbera and Nebbiolo. In 1875 Francisco Vidiella introduced the variety Folle Noire in an area called Colon, while Pascual Harriague planted the variety Tannat, which is also known as Harriague or Arraiga in Salto. The incorporation of Tannat is one of the most significant acts to have affected the small but noble Uruguayan wine industry, as it has allowed them to create a characteristic wine now considered emblematic of Uruguay. These tannic, smooth, and unusual wines express themselves on their own, but are also an excellent complement in blends with noble varieties such as Cabernet Sauvignon, Merlot, and Cabernet France.

The appellations of Uruguayan wines are subject to a specific and rigorously upheld decree called *Vinos de Calidad Preferente* (VCP: Preferred Quality Wines), controlled by the *Instituto Nacional de Vitivinicultura* (INAV: National Vitivinicultural Institute). As of the year 2000, the annual per capita consumption had reached 33 liters and the total production bordered on 100,000 liters, produced from 10,000 hectares. Uruguay, which is comparable in some ways to New Zealand, represents a nice example of how a small country can occupy a prestigious place in the world of wine.

Peru

At the height of its vitivinicultural peak, Peru reached 40,000 hectares of vineyards, which generated very good export-quality wines sold throughout Latin America and even Europe. However, the invasion of phylloxera in the late 19th century produced an impact that saw the vineyards converted to cotton plantations. There were attempts to revive the industry in the 1960s, but with little success. Peru currently has 11,000 hectares planted to vine and experimental stations in Ica, Chincha, Moquegua, and Tacna. Of the three primary vitivinicultural zones: the coast, the inter-Andean mountain area, and the jungle, the first is the most important. The grapes grown in these regions are largely Pisco varieties (*Negra Corriente, Italia, Moscatel,* and *Torontel*) and to a lesser degree vinifera varieties such as Chardonnay, Sauvignon Blanc, Chenin, Viognier, and Semillon in whites and Cabernet Sauvignon, Malbec, Merlot, Tannat, and Petit Verdot in reds.

Mexico

Mexican vitivinicultural development has proven both difficult and complex. The process of political independence ended the war that brought with it the nearly total destruction of its vineyards, which later increased with the US invasion of the northern territories, the fall of Emperor Maximilian, and the Reform War. These events accompanied the slow decline of the wine industry, a situation that was maintained through the coming decades.

In the late 19th century, the Livermore Valley based Concannon family stood out as pioneers in Californian vitiviniculture. As a direct consequence of their intervention before the Mexican government, Mexican vitiviniculture was encouraged, and more than a dozen French varieties were introduced. Years later in 1904, Concannon left Mexico and was succeeded by Perelló Minetti, who planted major extensions of vineyards close to Torreón 4 years later. The arrival of phylloxera in the early 20th century destroyed a large part of the Mexican vineyards. It is therefore believed that the true development of the wine industry did not begin until the 1917 revolution, although it was weak and very limited in scope. The crop was developed around Sonora, Baja California, and Zacatecas, followed by La Laguna, Aguas Calientes, and other areas. California Zinfandel was introduced in Baja California around 1925 and in Sonora between 1963 and 1967. Although Mexico was one of the first places in the Americas that European vines prospered and one of the first colonies to make wine, today it is known as a major brandy producer with a level of consumption that is much higher than rum and tequila, and Allied Domecq leads the industry with its state of the art facilities.

UNITED STATES

During the 19th century the United States significantly increased its territory by annexing areas such as California, which was later transformed into the center of vitivinicultural development. However, it is not the only area where vineyards have been planted; other regions with history and unique characteristics include New York, Ohio, Virginia, Florida, Washington, Oregon, Tennessee, North Carolina, Georgia, and Mississippi.

One of the pioneers of the country's vitivinicultural development was Jean Louis Vignes, who planted the first European vines in 1833 in his vineyard called *"El Aliso Vineyard"* outside Los Angeles. In the following years other colonists began to plant vineyards, encouraged by the increase in demand for food and drink generated by the Gold Rush.

Another noteworthy immigrant of the times was Agoston Haraszthy, who was sent to Europe to study vitiviniculture and bring back new varieties, including the now-emblematic Zinfandel. He was one of the first to request the creation of a School of Agriculture, which later incorporated the Department of Viticulture of Berkeley University. This outstanding personality also had the foresight to begin the research on the use of different American oaks for making barrels used to age and store wine. Viticulturist George Yount, recognized as one of the first to encourage the development of Napa Valley, introduced the vine to the valley when he planted the Mission grape in 1862.

Around 1860 vine growing had spread to other regions such as Ohio, Arkansas, North Carolina, Indiana, Missouri, and Tennessee, and later to Texas, New Mexico, and Florida. However, the inauguration of the transcontinental railway in 1869 allowed the commercialization of California wines in the eastern and mid-western states. Those factors, added to the conditions of the earth, soil, and climate allowed California to quickly surpass Missouri and Ohio and become the country's primary wine producer.

The vitivinicultural expansion in the U.S., particularly in California, was affected by the presence of phylloxera in Sonama, Napa, Solano, Yolo, Placer, and El Dorado counties. While some maintain that this was introduced in 1871, others suggest that phylloxera was already present in Sonoma twenty years earlier.

Around the end of the 19th century, the phylloxera problem was under control, and winemakers began to incorporate new technologies that allowed them to make better-quality wines and increase their vineyard acreage. Major contributions to vine growing and vinification processes began around 1880 through the University of California, which initiated a research program that continues today.

The state of Kansas enacted the country's first dry law around 1880, a trend the rest of the country would follow from 1920 to 1933. Under "Prohibition", wine production was strictly limited to wines destined for sacramental or medicinal use or those with special flavors for culinary use.

The Wine Institute was founded in California in 1936 and brought with it the creation of regulations for the potability and labeling of wine. Shortly thereafter in 1939, Frank Schoonmaker successfully fought for the use of varietal names on wine labels, a practice still in effect today.

Around 1950, wine experienced a reawakening when U.S. Soldiers returning from Europe after World War II brought back a taste for wine and aperitifs that caught on at home. The American Society of Enologists was formed around this time as well. By 1979, developments in North American vitiviniculture brought about the creation of the AVA (Approved Viticultural Area) appellation system that defines wine regions by their complexity, heterogeneity, and geographic extension.

The development of US vitiviniculture is intimately related to California, which in turn is linked to Chile. Despite being located in different continents and separated by 8,000 kilometers (or nearly 5,000 miles), there are a number of similarities between the two countries in terms of geography, history, and evolutionary origins. There are two objectives for establishing these connections: that readers knowledgeable of Chilean vitiviniculture better understand the Californian wine industry, and that those who know California reach a better understanding of Chile.

Chile's wine regions extend between 27° and 39° latitude south, while California's are 32° to 42° latitude north. However, if we limit its longitude strictly to the areas with clear vitivinicultural aptitudes, we find a great similarity, augmented by their shared climactic characteristics: rains concentrated in the winter and spring, followed by dry summer and autumn seasons. These conditions generate a close dependency on irrigation in both wine regions, categorically differentiating them from Europe.

Both coasts are bathed by cold currents: Chile by the Humboldt Current from the South Pole and California by the continuation of the Alaskan Current from the North Pole, in both cases resulting in an average diurnal temperature differential of approximately 20°C, with fluctuations that vary between 12° and 32°C, a phenomenon caused by cold air from the sea entering inland. Both regions have relatively low coastal mountain ranges that do not interrupt the marine air flows and high interior mountains, the Andes and the Rocky Mountain Ranges, that play a decisive role in the vineyard. These circumstances generate a parallel of applicable comparison that can present exceptions and specific cases that differ between the two regions.

Historically speaking, while there are variations in the genesis, there are also significant similarities beginning in the 19th century. While Fray Francisco de Carabantes introduced winegrowing in Chile in 1548, the Californian industry began 200 years later when Fray Junipero Serra introduced the vine, also for sacramental reasons. The first *Vitis vinifera sativa* variety to enter both countries was the same grape, called País in Chile and Mission in California.

The 1920 prohibition on alcohol added to the problems the U.S. wine industry already had with the expansion of phylloxera. The dry law was repealed in California in 1932.

Beyond this initial stage, the two countries shared several landmark moments, such as the importation of European varieties in the mid-19th century and the later participation of Chileans in the California Gold Rush, which began in 1850, as described in the notable work by Vicente Pérez-Rosales, *Recuerdos del Pasado* (Memories of the Past). It is reasonable to assume that coming from a country where viticulture had been a time-honored activity for more than three centuries, more than a few of the many Chilean immigrants in California in those years must have grown vines.

The wine industry improved with the participation of French winemakers and architects who began to arrive along with the European varieties. The result of the technical schools that they proposed is that both countries adhere to very similar vitivinicultural cannons, which remains true today. This development was accompanied by the introduction of new technologies, including the railroad, which in Chile's case was decisive for the development of the wine industry. Very close in time, the U.S. transcontinental railroad was inaugurated in 1869, which allowed California to become the country's primary wine producer. Those were also the years in which the first attempts at vitivinicultural research through the University of California and the Ministry of Agriculture in Chile's Quinta Normal.

The United States in general, and of course Californian vitiviniculture in particular, were damaged by the application of the Prohibition. Although Chile was never subjected to such a radical plan, its vitiviniculture suffered a series of erroneous economic policies that had negative effects when put into practice.

The character of Californian and Chilean wines has developed independently, although except for the respective varieties considered emblematic, such as Carmenère in Chile and Zinfandel in California, the industries share a greater incidence of red varieties over white, including the classic red varieties Cabernet Sauvignon, Cabernet Franc, and Merlot, and white varieties Sauvignon Blanc and Chardonnay.

The relationship is reinforced by the similarities that have ultimately been established between Chile's Casablanca Valley and California's Napa Valley, both marked by the strong influence of the Pacific Ocean. This similarity, observed by viticulturists who share projects in the two valleys, gave rise to a plan that sought a bond between the two regions, and in 2002 representatives of the two "Sister Cities" met in Napa Valley to sign not only a vitivinicultural union, but an exchange of culture and tourism as well.

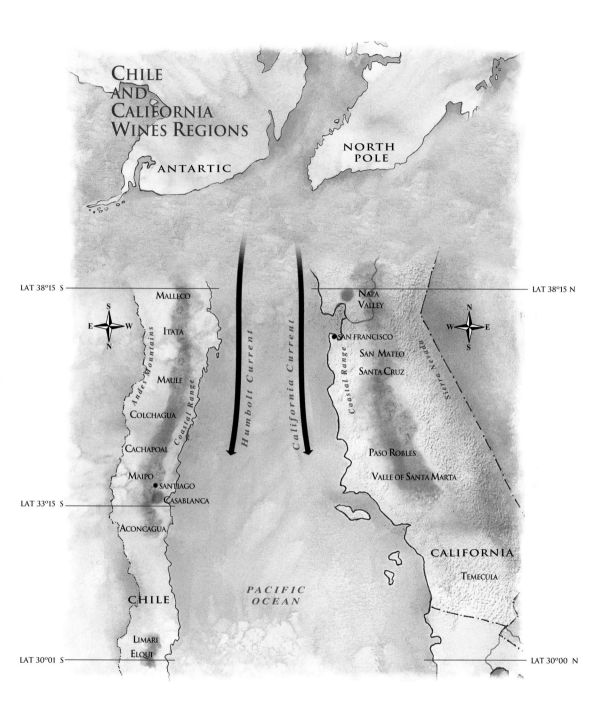

CHILE AND CALIFORNIA WINES REGIONS

NORTH POLE

ANTARTIC

LAT 38°15 S

MALLECO

Andes Mountains

ITATA

MAULE

COLCHAGUA

Coastal Range

CACHAPOAL

MAIPO

• SANTIAGO

CASABLANCA

LAT 33°15 S

ACONCAGUA

CHILE

LIMARI

ELQUI

LAT 30°01 S

Humbolt Current

California Current

PACIFIC OCEAN

LAT 38°15 N

NAPA VALLEY

• SAN FRANCISCO

SAN MATEO

Coastal Range

SANTA CRUZ

Sierra Nevada

PASO ROBLES

VALLE OF SANTA MARTA

CALIFORNIA

TEMECULA

LAT 30°00 N

AUSTRALIA

PERTH

GREAT SOUTHERN
REGION

RIVERLAND

BAROSSA

COONAWARRA

VICTORIA

HUNTER
VALLEY

SYDNEY

PACIFIC
OCEAN

MELBOURNE

N

TASMANIA
HOBART

144

Australia

Australia enters into the wine scene in 1788, with the arrival of the first vine stalks from Rio de Janeiro and Cape Town, which were established in Farm Cove, sometime after the Port Jackson Prison was founded. However, Australian vitivinicultural expansion was part of a slow process that achieved its first successful results in Parramata in 1816, with the vines brought from the Cape. The primary proponents of Australian vitiviniculture were John Macarthur from 1815 and Scottish immigrant James Busby beginning in 1824. They gave life to new vineyards in the New South Wales region, especially in Hunter Valley. Australia's southern territories were incorporated into wine growing in 1829 and Victoria around 1840. Added to the late introduction of the vine was the high consumption of beer and spirits. Australia was one of the few places in which livestock, especially sheep farming, offered better economic prospects than winegrowing. However, the British presence helped the expansion of the vineyards, as Napoleon Bonaparte's rise to power prevented the British Empire from continuing to receiving its supply of French wine. This in turn provided incentive for the English to turn Australia into the "Great British Vineyard." One of the serious crises that later affected wine production was the arrival of phylloxera in 1875, encompassing almost all of Oceania, with the exception of New South Wales.

With respect to the quality of Australian wines, the record indicates that early efforts focused on rustic fortified wines until the first part of the 20th century. The situation changed drastically around 1950 when developmental policies for fine wine production were applied, and a close collaborative wine management and research relationship was formed between the government and private enterprise. The result is that Australia now leads the New World in wine production and is the fourth largest exporter in the world, surpassing Chile, which is fifth. Along with this well-earned position, Australia's wine industry is known for the excellent varietal composition in its vineyards, its emblematic variety Shiraz, its development of new technologies, and its significant contributions in the field of viticulture, making it a true world-class model.

The Penfolds Wines company has represented the innovative spirit of the Australian wine industry in recent decades. Located in the Barossa Valley, with 6,000 hectares under vine, it is best known for its exclusive Grange Hermitage.

NEW ZEALAND

Anglican missionary Samuel Marsden introduced the vine to New Zealand in 1819, although the first wines were not made until 1832 by James Busby. Phylloxera hit the island in the late 19th century, prompting the replacement of *Vitis vinifera sativa* with hybrids, an error that was only rectified 60 years later when *Vitis vinifera* was reintroduced. This change began a new stage in the New Zealand wine industry, aided by the successful production of fine wines in 1960 and the introduction of Sauvignon Blanc and Pinot Noir, especially on South Island.

Paradoxically, from the point of view of its vineyard extension, New Zealand has a rather secondary importance, as even today it has less than 9,000 hectares of vineyard. In quality, however, this small country makes some of the world's best Sauvignon Blancs and other white wines, as well as a small amount of interesting Pinot Noir. Furthermore, New Zealand shares a curious geographical relationship with Chile, as the vitivinicultural region on this island is located between 33° and 53° latitude south, its northern limit corresponding to the Chilean city of Valdivia.

SOUTH AFRICA

South Africa's vitiviniculture suffered major setbacks with the arrival of phylloxera in 1880. This determined the need to rebuild the original vineyards and adapt them to the new structures of the world market, giving rise to the KWW Cooperative (*Kooperative Wijnbowers Vereniging van Zuid-Afrika*) in 1918, which became a powerful developmental factor in the country. The work of the KWW helped strengthen the old Stellenbosh and Nederburg farms, bought by the Monis family, and stimulated the creation of a semi-sweet while wine called Lieberstein that was so well received in Europe that it became the basis of South African vitivinicultural development. Other contributions of the KWW include the creation of an intra-specific hybrid cross between Pinot Noir and Cinsaut or Hermitage, which resulted in Pinotage, South Africa's emblematic variety.

Beginning in 1973, the application of a certification system of wines along with the major political restructuring that resulted in the end of Apartheid transformed the country into one of the primary New World producers and an important exporter, with the United Kingdom primsrily to. With vineyards near Cape Town, the country's best known region is Stellenboch. Today, South Africa has more than 120,000 hectares of vineyards, 15% of which are dedicated to red wines, mostly Pinotage. Other successfully-grown varieties include Cinsaut, Cabernet Sauvignon, Shiraz, and Pinot Noir.

CHILEAN VITIVINICULTURE
Globalization of Chilean Wine

The anxious search to produce fine wines has led to the discovery of new terroirs. One celebrated example is the Casablanca Valley, whose proximity to the Pacific Ocean creates ideal conditions for white varieties such as Sauvignon Blanc and Chardonnay.

The end of World War II brought with it a period of accelerated technological growth that extended well beyond the borders of Europe and the United States. This change marked significant milestones in industrial modes of production, transportation, communication, and commerce. Modernity and the international conflicts that accompanied it reached territories that were increasingly distant from centers of power, reproducing there part of their productive systems, economic aspirations, and cultural objectives.

Early in the second half of the 20th century, the world wine industry progressed toward a common horizon, ordered by their particular histories and by the rhythm of each region. Wine consumption during this period was restricted primarily to producer countries, such as France, Italy, and Spain, which had very high internal per capita consumption levels. The French, for example, consumed 100 liters per person per year until 1960.

Until 1970, only 8-10% of world's wine production was internationally marketed, and 80% of that trade took place between European countries. The participation of non-European countries in this market was practically non-existent. At that time Chile exported no more than 1% of its total production. The amount increased to just 5% during the 1980s, which in itself is very significant, considering that today Chile exports more than 60% of its production, a true world record.

As a consequence of the end of World War II and the slow increase of globalization of commercial, social, and political activities, new territories came onto the scene and ended Europe's monopoly on wine. The appearance of the United States as a modern and innovative producer represented a great contribution to the progress of world wide viticulture and winemaking with new technologies and research potential. Australia and South Africa followed close behind. The new contributions were expressed primarily in the development of winemaking based on sanitary practices and the absence of chemical products. The use of physical agents, strict hygiene in every step of the productive chain, and temperature-controlled fermentations in the case of white wines, gave rise to very high quality products.

This context generated a new trend in the United States in the 1960s. Wines were classified by variety and promoted as aperitifs in order to reach new consumers and reinforce the image of wine as a luxury item. This increased demand and stimulated the development of certain productive regions that reached international fame, such as California's Napa Valley and Chile's Casablanca Valley.

Despite its low internal consumption of approximately 8 liters per person per year, the United States maintains its position as world leader in technological developments. Research conducted by prestigious universities and research centers have allowed a balanced management of vineyards and the improvement of irrigation technology.

Attractive marketing plans developed in the U.S., Australia, and to a lesser degree South Africa and New Zealand, have changed the traditional European structure based on tradition, the mystique of the art of winemaking, and complicated appellation systems. Along with promoting the internationalization of wine and reinforcing its association with a more demanding consumer, a slow decrease in per capita consumption has taken place, explained by competition from an increased consumption of beer, high-quality spirits, carbonated soft drinks, coffee, and dairy products.

However, while overall wine consumption has dropped, interest in and demand for fine wines has increased, generating an interesting niche in the international market for new producer countries such as Chile, United States, New Zealand, Australia, and South Africa. The presence of New World producers and the redistribution of world production levels have affected the European industry, particularly France, which has seen its historic hegemony threatened and has been forced to institute changes in order to face new challenges.

STAGNATION PERIOD: 1950 – 1980

While European vitivinicultural activity was reborn after the war and a select group of fine wine producers from Australia, South Africa, and New Zealand entered the scene with state-of-the-art technology, most Latin American wine-producing countries were experiencing stagnated economies. The exception was Argentina, which enjoyed a strong economy at that time. It was an industry leader based on its very high unit production, large extensions of vineyards, and a high internal rate of consumption. However, this privileged situation became unfavorable over the long term, due to a lack of concern for the production of fine wines.

To the west of the Andes, Chile recovered slowly from the impact of the 1939 Alcohol Law. The 1950s began a relatively stable market, a flowing wine industry in the hands of the Vicuña Mackenna Catalonians, and a process of stagnation and decadence in the traditional wineries, with the exception of Concha y Toro, Undurraga, Santa Carolina, and San Pedro.

By the 1930s the government had positioned itself at the center of the national development project, instituting an economic plan to recover the depressed Chilean industry. A program was proposed that provided incentives for State participation in every area of the economy, particularly in a policy of substituting imports that sought to strengthen national industrialization. This context of intervention coincided with international post-World War II programs for economic reconstruction by reducing dependence on external markets. Limitations on imports reduced foreign machinery in the hopes of encouraging internal production and national industrial development, making vitivinicultural production process more difficult and expensive.

The economic criteria of self-sufficiency and the elimination of importation of capital goods and raw materials drove the industry toward obsolescence and stagnation, while the opposite began taking place among its future competitors in post-war Australia, New Zealand, United States, and South Africa.

In Chile, local conditions prevented the renovation of winemaking facilities and forced the use of inappropriate woods, such as *raulí* or Chilean oak (*Nothofagus alpine*) for wine containers. The wood imparted negative flavors to the wine, and although local consumers were accustomed to it, the foreign market rejected it, creating an obstacle to Chilean wine in the international market that was not resolved until the 1990s.

Most Chilean wine was distributed internally in *chuicos* (15 liters), demijohns (10 liters), or jugs (5 liters); no more than 1% of the total production was released in 700cc bottles. One-liter bottles made their first appearance in 1964, pioneered by the Concha y Toro and Santa Teresa wineries.

Modifications began to take place in the wineries during this period. For example, Concha y Toro, which had incorporated in 1923, obtained the representation of Coca Cola in Chile in 1940. Viña San Pedro had a network of wineries and warehouses from Arica to Punta Arenas. Viña Undurraga was a pioneer in exporting Chilean wine thanks to the efforts of Pedro Undurraga, who crossed the Panama Canal with sample bottles. Although our national wine was quite mediocre at the time, Undurraga distributed his throughout the world. The world map in his office provides evidence: 50 flags represent the countries in which he managed to sell his product. As the father of massive exports, he had the foresight to create the Wine Exporters Consortium and encourage its fusion with the Bottlers Association to form what is now the Viñas de Chile trade organization.

It is interesting to note the work of Genovese immigrant José Canepa, who first arrived in Chile in the early 1900s. He created a wine distributorship in Valparaíso, which soon led to winegrowing and producing in the community of Isla de Maipo, where he planted and developed large vineyards, along the banks of the Maipo River. He also had olive groves in Curicó.

Vitivinicultural cooperatives formed in the 1940s in Cauquenes, Talca, and Curicó. The first was the Cooperativa Agrícola Vitivinícola de Cauquenes Ltda. (COVICA), formed to aid local growers who needed to vinify their grapes after the devastating earthquake of 1939 had destroyed the existing winery facilities. Other cooperatives included Loncomilla, Linares, Ñuble, Quillón, and Coelemu. With State support, they reached their peak as an organizational system in the 1970s, when they represented 15% of the national production.

The State's interest in entering the wine industry became clear during the government of President Pedro Aguirre Cerda, with the 1941 creation of VINEX, the *Sociedad Vinos de Chile* (Chilean Wine Association). Its major objectives were to show that the Chilean government was capable of exporting national wines, as well as regulating the market on occasion. Neither intention lasted, and its management ended with the onset of the military government in 1973 when VINEX was assigned to the Wagner and Stein company after a public bidding process.

Wine exports during the 1950s were limited and remained constant until 1958, when international sales increased dramatically due to the exportation of 52 million liters to France, an enormous amount sent in answer to the crisis of supply as a consequence of the French war with Algeria. Unfortunately, the wines were unable to meet the standards of quality expected by the French consumer, and a great opportunity to enter the European market was lost.

During this time a process of renovation took place that promoted the formation of vitivinicultural organizations and associations. In the technical area, it is important to mention the creation of the National Association of Agricultural Engineers-Enologists, founded in 1953 and presided over by Ruy Barbosa until 1968. A series of associations was formed in the commercial and agricultural areas to promote vitivinicultural exchange and improve the industry.

In the 1950s, the profession of agricultural engineer incorporated a new specialization in enology, and thus Chile's first enologists conferred status and hierarchy upon the activity that would contribute to the technological progress of Chilean wine. Curricular changes were introduced to improve the training of students. The Catholic University of Chile created specializations in Fruiticulture and Vitiviniculture within the agricultural program. International networks and alliances were formed that allowed some recently-graduated agricultural engineers to pursue post graduate enological studies in France, primarily in Montpellier and Bordeaux, producing a significant renovation in the approach to the discipline in Chile.

On the international scale, the decade of the 1970s was characterized by technological advances in the industry's leading countries. Vitiviniculture experienced major enological progress. Chile, however, remained stagnant with respect to wine, despite the changes introduced at the educational, associative, and technical levels. One of the attempts to improve the industry took place within the framework of the Latin American Free Trade Association, which allowed machinery to be imported from Argentina. In this context, the issue of taxes continued to be a matter of concern for wine producers. The National Viticultural Association proposed, as one of its primary objectives, the repeal of the Wine Production Tax and the law that restricted the plantation of vineyards. The Association won their fight, and the tax was replaced by an increase in the rate of the Purchase and Sales Tax. However, this provoked chaos in the industry because it allowed high rates of evasion, as much as 50% in the central-south region of the country.

The Agrarian Reform project, enacted as law in August 1962 under the government of President Jorge Alessandri, not only instituted a structural change in the tenancy of the land, but also launched a virtual revolution in the traditional agrarian structure and a lack of confidence in the future of the sector, which halted agricultural investment. These conditions caused a decrease in cultivated land and the stagnation of commercial exchange at a time when competing countries were increasing their vineyards, technified the productive process, and increased commerce.

During the 1960s, international academic and commercial contacts encouraged visits by distinguished experts, such as French Professor Denis Boublas, of the Montpellier University, and Wilhem Gärtel, German director of the Berkastel Kues Botanical and Vitivinicultural Institute, who lent significant technical assistance. Also noteworthy are Professor Mario Fregoni, of the Italian University of Piacenza, who proposed that UNESCO declare Chilean vitiviniculture a *World Heritage Site*, and French ampelographer Jean Michel Boursiquot, who was decisive in the identification of the variety Carmenère in the mid-1990s. Also worthy of mention are Ignacio Lauterbach (German) and Luciano Bally (French), both now deceased, along with two still-practicing German winemakers, Goetz von Gersdorff and Klaus Schroeder, who settled in Chile in the 1950s and 1960s, respectively.

Among the younger generations who broke ground in the development of Chilean vitivinicultural activity, we should mention Agustín Huneeus, who contributed to turning Viña Concha y Toro into an industry leader. He later emigrated to the United States, where he brilliantly managed the Seagram Corporation's vitivinicultural concerns. He later established himself as an independent in the famous Napa Valley, where he has become a true leader in U.S. vitiviniculture, an example he exported to Chile when he formed the Viña Veramonte in the Casablanca Valley.

The political situation of the 1970s awakened a strong opposition on the part of those who opposed the programs of President Salvador Allende. The Agrarian Reform Plan accelerated without the approval of the Chilean Association of Wine Bottlers and Exporters, which led the organization to distance itself through organizations such as SOFOFA (Society of Industrial Promotion) and the Confederation of Production and Commerce. The plan chosen by the Association was an approach to the government to be able to expand the terms of the negotiations, as they had no confidence in the permanency of Allende's Popular Unity government. The new productive structure of the wineries proposed by the government never went into effect due to the political changes that took place in Chile on September 11, 1973.

The political and economic instability of the early 1970s along with changes in the habits of the Chilean people had a significant effect on the wine industry. Television, the increase in advertising, and the generalized use of refrigerators increased the consumption of beer and soft drinks, generating a dramatic decrease in wine consumption, not only in Chile, but world wide.

The first definite "Argentinization" of Chilean vitiviniculture occurred during those years, and plantations destined for mass production of common wines were increased. This situation lasted for some 15 years and generated a dramatic reduction in the wine sector. The military government refrained from intervening, arguing that the so-called automatic adjustment should operate in the market economy. This economic policy is reflected in a famous comment made by a politician of the time who responded to a complaint from members of the dairy industry about the lack of market for milk by saying, *"Eat the cows."*

There were many arguments of this type on the part of the authorities with respect to the wine industry, and this explains why the 106,000 hectares of vineyards that had existed in 1974 dwindled to 54,000 by 1994. The expected automatic adjustment finally took place and brought with it major socio-economic difficulties, especially for small and medium-sized producers. Plantations of common varieties such as País and Moscatel dropped abruptly decrease from 60,000 to 20,000 hectares. Maintaining the structure of free market, the Decree Law 2753 was created in 1979 to modify the 1939 Alcohol Law. This new legal scenario initiated a true disaster in the vitivinicultural sector due to the suppression of winery-related regulatory legislation that authorized the hybrid grape varieties (also known as direct producers) and eliminated the legal function of agricultural engineer-enologists.

The Chilean Wine Boom: 1980 – 2004

After the wine industry's long period of stagnation, the 1980s symbolized the beginning of a series of changes that began to completely modify the production of Chilean wines. This period was marked by the presence of national and international investors who took over some of the traditional family wineries and started up new winery projects. The modernization of winery facilities and the introduction of improvements in the winemaking process allowed the increase of production and the opening of new export markets. The attraction of wine was accompanied by the rediscovery of varieties such as Carmenère, wich allowed the continuation of the diversification of production and generated attractive markets tied to specific varieties.

Additional current developments include original horizons that have emerged in the industry in relation to tourism, wine routes, culinary circuits, and the interesting work of sommeliers. This progress promoted an increase in both production and exportation, which in turn has allowed Chilean wine to enter a greater number of countries.

The growth of the importation of wooden barrels (from US$1.48 million in 1990 to US$15 million in 2003) explains the increase in national production and the quality of wine. Exports of bottled wine rose from 36 million units in 1990 to 325 million in 2003. Bulk wine exports increased from 14.6 million liters to 161 million liters, an increase from US$6.1 million to US$88 million. Thus the participation of exports of Chilean wine in the world market rose 5.4 times, from 0.96% in 1990 to 5.3% in 2003. The growth trend has been maintained, and new wineries with state-of-the-art facilities and excellent designs have been created.

This growth is situated within private initiatives, partially coordinated by the *Asociación de Viñas de Chile* (Association of Chilean Wineries) and *Chile Vid*. Participation in international fairs and commercial missions, partially financed by Pro Chile, has also been essential for promoting Chilean wine abroad. These initiatives, along with new investments, explain how Chile came to be the fifth largest wine exporter in the world, surpassed only by France, Italy, Spain, and Australia. This spectacular progress is situated within the context of the international development that has affected countries such as the United States, Australia, New Zealand, and South Africa.

The New World's success has awakened Europea to the need to strengthen it's industry, thereby creating new challenges for Chilean wine to remain in the position it earned during the 1990s. However, the national scenario has already presented certain problems. The internal wine market dropped sharply in favor of beer and pisco. National per capita consumption fell from 42.7 liters per year in 1980 to a low of 13.1 liters in 1997. The figure has since risen somewhat to 16.2 liters in 2003. Beer consumption, however, rose from 16.5 liters per capita in 1985 to 27 liters in 2001, while pisco rose from 1,5 to 2,65 liters during the same period.

Another negative factor related to the expectations that wine stimulates is the irrational increase of wine grape plantations, which have increased 101%, from 54,000 hectares in 1994 to 108,562 in 2003. This figure clearly upsets the market, encourages the appearance of irregular parallel markets, and lowers the price of Chilean wine at home and abroad.

It is difficult to place blame in this context, but it points to the fact that investors, business consultants, and economists lack adequate knowledge of the history of wine and the phenomenon of excess supply as a chronic and cyclical problem that dates back to ancient times. This lack of knowledge is what validates efforts such as this book, in which the history of Chilean wine is inserted into a broad chronological framework in relation to the world, no longer from the perspective of historiography, but rather from that of the protagonists.

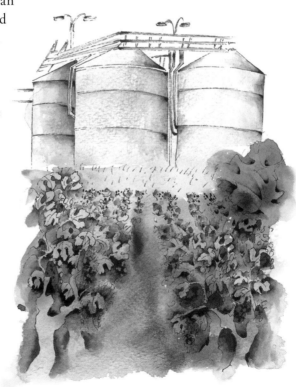

Well-known Napa Valley vintner Robert G. Mondavi formed a partnership with Eduardo Chadwick of Viña Errázuriz. Together they incorporated modern technology and a particular form of vineyard management that gave rise to Seña, the exclusive wine that forms part of Chile's select group of premium wines.

Foreign Influence

In the late 1970s, a young Catalonian winemaker named Miguel Torres arrived in Chile. He acquired a small piece of land in Curicó and set about to do what Chilean winemakers had only dreamed of; he made modern wines that could compete at the international level thanks to the introduction of technology and state-of-the art facilities. Torres became one of the pioneers of modern Chilean winemaking, because despite their theoretical knowledge of the latest innovations, not a single winery had invested in stainless steel tanks, elements that allowed temperature-controlled fermentations, or in new American or French oak barrels.

The presence of foreign capital brought with it technological changes that followed the path laid out by Torres for importing stainless steel and high-tech equipment. The first harvest under the new conditions produced wines that were fresh, aromatic, and fruity–and heartily rejected by local consumers, who declared them undrinkable. Torres, however, was not deterred by the criticism. His product was well-received abroad, and his style quickly became the new norm in Chile, a trend that continues to the present.

Following Miguel Torres' example, the Guilisasti family began to develop a positive investment plan and an active modernization of the Concha y Toro company. The family patriarch, Eduardo Guilisasti, president of the company from the 1960s until his death in the 1990s, laid the foundations for transforming Concha y Toro into Chile's most important winery. It was the first winery to sell stock on Wall Street, which intensified its future success and led it to become the top-selling foreign wine brand in the United States.

Other major parties began to enter the wine business, assuming the process of modernization and technification. Ricardo Claro acquired Viña Santa Rita and Viña Carmen in the mid-1980s; the Cruzat Larraín group took over Viña Santa Carolina and Viña San Pedro, while others, still without declaring their definitive owners, showed clear signs of progress.

In 1982 Viña Canepa, founded in 1930 by José Canepa, began building a modern winery with the latest vinification and bottling equipment. His example was quickly followed by other wine companies, such that by the late 1980s, Chile was in condition to offer internationally competitive wines for first time. This scenario born of a privileged climate, select varieties, ultra-modern facilities, and well-trained professionals allowed the improvement of fine wine production. Unfortunately, as historian José del Pozo has pointed out, the unsuspected quality of these new wines did not have the international impact it deserved due to the embargos imposed by international markets against the Pinochet regime.

Apalta and Ninquén, in the Colchagua Valley, stand out for producing high-quality wines of exceptional character. Hillside vineyards, now possible thanks to drip irrigation, are one of the most important factors contributing to the quality of these new terroirs. Viña Montes La Finca de Apalta vineyard.

The presence of other foreigners continued to maintain Chilean wine production fresh and up-to-date. The French company Les Domains Barons de Rothschild (Lafite) established itself in Chilean vitiviniculture in 1988. They bought Viña Los Vascos on the old Cañeten Hacienda in Peralillo, in the Colchagua Valley, which they improved by initiating a modernization and investment program in which their savoir faire would lead them to obtain high quality wines.

Another branch of the Rothschild family, led by the Baroness Philippine de Rothschild, associated with Viña Concha y Toro in 1997 and formed the Viña Almaviva, which gives name to its primary product.

The Almaviva concept follows the standard of production of the great French wines called Grand Crus Classé, known as *Primer Orden* (First Order) in Chile. This strict level of quality allowed Almaviva to be the only wine produced outside of Bordeaux to form part of the French system of sales through négociants, thereby inserting itself in the elite world of wine. The Almaviva winery, which is a work of art in itself, vinifies its 42 hectares of vineyards, carefully attending to each step of the process, from the soil and irrigation to ageing and bottling, to ensure the birth of its great wine.

Almaviva exemplifies the trend of fine wine producers dedicated to making one great and unique wine from a single vineyard and in an exceptional winery facility.

The members of the Rothschild family are not the only French winemakers who chose to invest in Chile. The famous Château Larose Trintaudon, wich belongs to the AGF/Allianz insurance company, associated with the Granella family in Chile to create the Las Casas del Toqui winery.

Another agreement between Chileans and foreigners gave life to Viña Casa Lapostolle, born of an association between the French Marnier family and the Chilean Rabat family. The Lapostolle's history in the production of alcoholic beverages dates back to 1827, when family moved to the Charente region and Alexandre Marnier-Lapostolle created the famous liqueur Grand Marnier, a blend of cognac and orange essence. More than 100 years later, Casa Lapostolle fulfilled the dream of producing fine wines in the New World under the direction of Alexandra Marnier-Lapostolle. The winery, now wholly-owned by the French family, has had great success, espeacially with its icon wine Clos Apalta.

In 1992, French producer William Fèvre, from Chablis, joined forces with Chilean partner Víctor Pino to form the association of Du Vignoble William Fèvre (France) and Viña William Fèvre (Chile), in the San Luis sector of Pirque in the Maipo Valley. Another interesting example of French investors is Viña Aquitania, originally formed by an association between Bruno Prats (of Château Cos-d'Estournel), Paul Pontallier (Château Margaux), and Chilean winemaker Felipe de Solminihac. This winery brings together Prats and Pontallier, two particularly relevant wine personalities and Felipe de Solminihac, with a meritorious career in wine and the current president of the Chilean *Cofradía al Mérito Vitivinícola* (Vitivinicultural Brotherhood of Merit).

The Massenez family, producers of Alsatian fruit brandies, moved to Chile and acquired Viña Santa Amalia. They transformed it into Château Los Boldos and have achieved very high quality wines.

Another example is Villard Fine Wines, a Casablanca Valley winery owned in large part by Thierry Villard, a French-born Australian wine producer. Villard has created extremely high quality wines that have contributed to the prestige of Chilean wine, especially in the Casablanca Valley. The Sociedad de Vignobles, comprised of Polynesian investors Michael Paoletti, Robert and Luis Wan, along with Julián Sin, has had a significant presence in the country. They make wine under the labels Domaine Oriental and Casa Donoso, constituting a large part of the creation of top quality wines in the Talca region (Maule Valley).

Also included among the distinguished foreign investors is North American Robert Mondavi, the famed Napa Valley producer, well known for his joint ventures with French vitiviniculturists. For example, Mondavi established a partnership with Baron Philippe de Rothschild in 1979, to create the now-famous Opus One, one of the first fine wines made in the Oakville area of California's Napa Valley. In 1995 he associated with the Chilean winery, Viña Errázuriz, owned by the Chadwick Errázuriz family, to jointly create Seña, a blend of Cabernet Sauvignon and Carmenère, which belongs of a select group of fine Chilean wines.

In 1997, North American Jess Jackson set up in Digua (Maule Valley) and began planting vineyards and building a vineyard near Talca, thus the Kendall-Jackson company took shape in Chile as the Calina Winery.

Another significant winery is Veramonte, property of Chilean-born, Napa Valley resident Agustín Huneeus. It currently generates top quality wines in the Casablanca Valley in co-ownership with one of the first and largest wine companies in North America, Constellation Wines, which has helped it to export large quantities of wine to the United States.

Chile's foreign investors are not limited to the North Americans, French, and Spaniards, however. The Norwegian Odfjell family fell in love with Chilean vitiviniculture and founded the beautiful Odfjell Vineyards, along the old route between Santiago and Valparaíso. In just a few years of activity, not only have they realized a dream but contributed extraordinary wines to the Chilean market.

The presence of foreign investors in Chile is also explained by the incorporation of the country into the international scenario in the 1990s. Their presence has not only provided a major economic contribution, but has constituted an assurance of the seriousness and stability of the Chilean market, along with the natural conditions that Chile offers for producing quality wines.

Alejandro Hernández, Agricultural Engineer-Enologist and Professor Emeritus of the Faculty of Agronomy of the Catholic University of Chile, deserves special mention. In 1994 he was elected president of the International Office of Vine and Wine (OIV), founded in 1924 and based in Paris. He was the first non-European to occupy the position, a true indication of the organization's esteem not only of Hernández, but of Chile as well.

The Discovery of Carmenère

Carmenère, also known as *Grande Vidure, Carmenelle, Cabernelle y Grant Carmenet*, was originally from the Medoc region of France. Toward the mid-20th century, before the outbreak of phylloxera, Carmenère arrived in Chile along with Cabernet Sauvignon, one of the varieties with the greatest prestige among the great Bordeaux wines. However, as a result of phylloxera's expansion throughout Europe, it was almost entirely abandoned, as grafting it over other *Vitis* varieties notably decreased its production.

In 1991, French ampelographer Claude Valat visited Chile to study the Merlot plantations, as he perceived that the character of Chilean Merlot wines did not correspond to the variety. The result of his observations partially identified some Merlot vineyards as Cabernet Franc, leaving open the interest in studying and discovering more about this variety. In 1994 his follower, Jean Michel Boursiquot of the ENSA in Montpellier, was invited to attend the 6th Latin American Congress on Viticulture and Enology. During his visits to vineyards and wineries, he identified the Merlot vineyard at Viña Carmen to be Carmenère. He later visited other wineries in the Metropolitan area and the southern valleys, questioning the traditional classification of some Merlots.

This stimulated an unusual interest that led to a number of studies animed at identifying the ampelographical characteristics and enological potential of the variety. The discovery also meant a considerable increase in the hectares of Carmenère, not only due to the reclassification of old vineyards, primarily located in Maule and Colchagua, but also to the new hectares being planted. The enthusiasm for

The grape variety Carmenère was long confused with Merlot until it was identified by French ampelographer Jean Michel Boursiquot in 1994. It later became one of Chile's emblematic varieties, along with Cabernet Sauvignon.

Carmenère was also fueled by a great interest in having an emblematic variety, such as Pinotage in South Africa, Syrah in Australia, Malbec in Argentina, and Zinfandel in California.

In 1994 Viña Carmen, under the enological direction of Alvaro Espinoza, was the first to vinify Carmenère as a new variety. It was released as Grande Vidure, a synonym of Carmenère, to avoid any confusion with the name Viña Carmen. They also had to overcome many problems due to the fact that the variety was not included in the official register of permitted varieties, as it had been considered extinct.

Viña Santa Inés De Martino (now Viña De Martino), however, launched the first wine labeled as Carmenère in 1996, made by winemaker Adriana Cerda.

Despite Carmenère's rise in popularity, Cabernet Sauvignon continues to be considered one of the most important varieties in the national vineyards. This Old World variety gave rise to Chile's first vineyards dedicated to fine wines in the Maipo Valley, through the efforts of traditional wineries such as Cousiño Macul, Concha y Toro, Santa Rita, and others. In time it became the most widely planted variety due to the international market's preference for red wine. A further benefit is that its thick skin makes it resistant to diseases, thereby allowing it to produce wines that are both economical and enjoyable.

The Great Fine Wines

The knowledge, technological improvements, and experience accumulated in the 1980s allowed winemakers to reach a level of quality never before achieved in Chile. This was possible thanks to the progressive acceptance of Chilean wine in the external market, which encouraged certain wineries equipped with the necessary technological and economic conditions to begin the ambitious task of creating superior quality wines for the international market.

Among the first wineries to venture into the production of premium wines were Concha y Toro, Montes, Casa Lapostolle, Errázuriz, and Almaviva. Their wines have been widely recognized, and in 2004 Almaviva and Casa Lapostolle's Clos Apalta each earned a coveted 95 points in Wine Spectator magazine.

Concha y Toro started the process in 1986 when it took its first steps toward realizing its dream of producing excellent quality wines that would be able to position Chile as a world-class fine wine producer. In 1987, Jacques Boissenot, a consultant to major French châteaux, began to direct the Don Melchor project along with winemaker Goetz von Gersdorff, adding Enrique Tirado to the team later on. Over time, Don Melchor, a Cabernet Sauvignon, Cabernet Franc, and Petit Verdot blend, has become a symbol of great Chilean fine wines. The wine is made from grapes from the Tocornal Fundo in Puente Alto in the Maipo Valley at the foot of the Andes Mountains, an area traditionally characterized as a generator of the highest quality Cabernet Sauvignon.

Concha y Toro's long history, as well as Don Melchor's 18 years of existence, allows us to observe part of the evolution of Chile's fine wines and their international acceptance, proof of which are the outstanding wine scores awarded by magazines such as Decanter, Wine Spectator, Wine Access, and others.

In 1988, the well-known winemaker Aurelio Montes and business partners Douglas Murray, Alfredo Vidaurre, and Pedro Grand founded Viña Montes. The winery stood out for being the first non-traditional winery dedicated solely to the production of excellent wines, topped by its now famous wine M, a blend of Cabernet Sauvignon, Cabernet Franc, Merlot, and Petit Verdot from the hillsides of Apalta in the Colchagua Valley. These facing slopes southwest are open to the

Chile's modern and complete wine shops offer the best national and foreign labels as well as wine books and accessories. They also include room for tastings and wine courses.

influence of coastal breezes that cool the natural heat of the region and contribute favorable conditions for red wines.

In 1994, the Colchagua Valley gave birth to another of its great wines: Clos Apalta, the product of the partnership between the French Marnier family, creators of the famous Grand Marnier, and the Chilean Rabat family. This wine, a blend of Carmenère, Merlot, Cabernet Sauvignon, and Malbec, very quickly occupied a place among Chile's exclusive group of great fine wines. Alexandra Marnier's dream was to produce an excellent New World wine, and no holds were barred in building a model winery and hiring the prestigious French flying winemaker Michel Rolland.

The 1995 joint venture between the traditional Viña Errázuriz and Robert Mondavi resulted in Seña, a wine born of the terroir of Ocoa, on the edge of the La Campana Hill, a World Biosphere Reserve. The first bottling, from the 1995 vintage, was released in early 1998, thus opening a new chapter in the development of the Chilean wine industry. Seña has combined the conditions of quality from the little niches of the Aconcagua Valley with excellent management, which has positioned it as one of Chile's select premium wines. Viñedo Chadwick, another Errázuriz wine, earned world recognition in 2004 when it took first place over a number of French wines in a major tasting in Berlin.

Almaviva, one of the most prestigious wineries of recent years, is located in Puente Alto. It originated through an alliance between Concha y Toro and Mouton-Rothschild in 1997, giving rise to the only Chilean wine that faithfully follows the Bordeaux Grand Cru Classé model, which refers to a winery and vineyard dedicated to producing one single wine. It is noteworthy that Almaviva, a blend of Cabernet Sauvignon, Carmenère, and Cabernet Franc, is the only non-Bordeaux wine distributed by French négociants.

The desire to produce fine wines is not limited to this select group of wineries, but rather forms part of a shared goal of all the wineries that seek prestige through quality. In 1985 Miguel Torres created its exclusive Manso de Velasco wine, followed by Santa Rita's Casa Real in 1989, Viña Carmen's Gold Reserve in 1993, Cousiño Macul's Finis Terrae (1996), Errázurriz's Don Maximiano (1996), Tarapacá's Milenium (1998), and Chadwick (1999), plus others from Undurraga and San Pedro. Top wines from newer wineries include Château Los Boldos' Grand Cru (1996), Clos Quebrada de Macul's Domus Aurea (1996), Antiyal (1998), and Morandé's House of Morandé (1999).

New wine regions have been discovered along the way, such as the now renowned Casablanca Valley, which produces excellent white wines such as Sauvignon Blanc and Chardonnay. The Casablanca Valley extends over approximately 4,000 hectares and is characterized by its maritime influence, responsible for the cold climate ideal for white wines. Chilean winemaker Pablo Morandé is credited with the 'discovery' of the valley in 1982, paving the way to the exploration of other new wine regions, such as Limarí in the north, Leyda and San Antonio along the coast, and colder areas such as Mulchén and Traiguén in the south. The search for new areas and exceptional terroirs branched out in all directions, and vineyards started to climb up the hillsides. The new philosophy is that wine is made in the vineyard, and every aspect of winegrowing is considered vitally important.

In winegrowing, terroir refers to a specific and limited space that combines a wide range of necessary factors, such as day- and night-time temperatures, soils, drainage, and protection from the wind, etc. This is not enough, however; new vineyards begin with the delimitation of the land and the selection of the variety and must then be carefully managed with human knowledge and intuition.

The Chilean Association of Sommeliers Association was created in 1997 to train experts in food, wine, and service. One of the major proponents of the organization is Héctor Vergara, Latin America's only Master Sommelier.

Gastronomy and Tourism

The wine boom has surpassed wine's traditional commercial sphere, allowing the rise of gastronomy, expert sommeliers, specialized magazines and wine writers, elegant wine shops, museums, and even hotels. The prestige earned by Chilean wines has sparked an interest in visiting the wineries, generating tour circuits and wine routes that offer wine-based recreational and educational experiences. The primary wine routes to date are found in Colchagua, Casablanca, Curicó, and Maule Valley.

This joint strategy aimed at publicizing Chilean wines and wine regions reflects one of the many steps taken to better position itself as a wine-producing country. The programs follow examples that originated in Europe and the United States, where the wine regions are open to anyone who wishes to visit, such as the exemplary Napa Valley, open to tourism year round, inviting the public to visit the wineries and other places of interest. A number of interesting initiatives are growing in Chile. Early examples include the wine routes in the Colchagua Valley and in Villa Alegre in San Javier (Maule Valley).

Improved services and the desire to show vineyard characteristics have generated new circuits, food and wine festivals, and other events. One such example is the Harvest Festival in the Curicó Valley, which has been held for close to 20 years. Another is the magnificent Colchagua Valley Harvest Festival, which takes place in early March and offers not only an excellent opportunity to promote the region's wines, but also celebrates the valley's culture, gastronomy, and history. These festivals have also spread to urban areas, especially Santiago, as a means of spotlighting the virtues of the country's different wine regions.

Many of Chile's vitivinicultural regions have Wine Routes that promote tourism through vineyards and wineries along with local cultural and natural attractions. The hospitality of the Chilean people is well-known and makes it easy for international visitors to make their way through the valleys on their own.

The Colchagua Valley is the heart and soul of country life in Chile's central zone and offers visits to wineries such as Casa Silva, Viu Manent, Casa Lapostolle, Montes, Bisquertt, and others through its Wine Route. Tours include a visit to the Colchagua Museum, one of the country's best, featuring a permanent collection that provides an overview of different historical periods, from pre-historic times to the present. It also presents colonial architecture and agricultural techniques, country apparel, religious objects, and transportation methods, all closely related to wine production and marketing.

The Hotel Santa Cruz Plaza was recently built across from the *Plaza de Armas* (the central square) in the Colchagua Valley town of Santa Cruz. Although new, the building respects the principles of local colonial architecture and is decorated with a wine-related theme.

CHILEAN WINE. THE HERITAGE

Not only has interest in fine wines from Chile and elsewhere promoted interest in wine tourism, but it has given rise to a number of specialized boutique-style wine shops as well. The first to open its doors was The Wine House, founded in 1993, followed by the Vinoteca in 1995. South America's largest wine shop, El Mundo del Vino, opened in 1999 and includes Héctor Vergara, Latin America's only Master Sommelier, among its founders. These shops are equipped with specialized personnel, members' clubs, wine courses, tastings, and winery visit programs.

Another recent phenomenon is Chile's rising interest in sommeliers. The Chilean Association of Sommeliers was created in 1997, which in turn created its Sommelier School in conjunction with the Chilean Gastronomic Association (ACHIGA). As of 2000, the school has provided training in correct methods to serve wine, attend customers, handle wine and other beverages, create wine lists, and the other responsibilities of the sommelier, with the aim of affirming the prestige and complexity of the culture of wine.

Sommeliers are true wine consultants, able to offer and recommend wine based on their vast knowledge of the product. Today it is an esteemed profession, dedicated to managing the basic arts of wine.

Hotel Santa Cruz Plaza is Chile's first 5-star, small-town hotel dedicated to providing services for winery visitors. It is located next to the Colchagua Museum, the country's most important private museum, which displays many objects in use when Chilean vitiviniculture began.

CHILEAN WINE. THE HERITAGE

Héctor Vergara is among the pioneers in these initiatives. He is a partner in the aforementioned Mundo del Vino and the associated enterprise Cavas Reunidas, and holds the coveted title of Master Sommelier, granted by the Court of Master Sommeliers in London. The contributions of Pascual Ibañez should also be mentioned. Trained in the Spanish School of Sommeliers, he arrived in Chile in the early 1990s and initiated his important work in opening the world of wine to the general public through education and culture.

Evidence of the increasing presence of sommeliers in restaurants is the availability of better wine lists with a broader range of selections, along with an increase in tasting courses and culinary festivals that reinforce the relationship between food and wine. These professionals in the art of wine have also become more available in supermarkets and specialized wine shops, guiding customers in their selections.

Wine has also come to play an important role in our society as a cultural catalyst, facilitating the connections between the different manifestations of art and literature. Chile's interest in learning about wine and its culture began as a trend, quickly became popular, and has slowly generated a refining factor in general society. This has been possible due to a broad range of excellent quality wines available at affordable prices, which has also led to a greater appreciation of gastronomy, an important indicator of a country's cultural development.

Rodrigo Alvarado
Santiago, Chile 2004

Epilogue

The Future of Chilean Wine?

Although it seems pretentious to make predictions about the future of our wine industry, the subject is inevitable. We would do well to remember that despite the sector's negative prognosis in the early 1990s, this is when the foundation was laid for the great hierarchy of Chilean vitivinicultural agro-industry.

The development of the 1990s was based on the concept of maintaining a ratio between price and quality. This relationship should not be abandoned by any means, but neither should Chilean wine be limited to this range; it must be complemented by the production of great fine wines in the 'Premium,' 'Ultra Premium,' and 'Icon' ranges as well. Good examples already exist in this area. They have been well-received in the market, and many of our wines now commonly receive scores of 90 points or higher in prestigious trade magazines around the world. On the other hand, we have many modern and highly functional wineries, some of which may even go overboard in their elegance, but they certainly push the entire sector.

Happily, new wine-related initiatives are developing, such as the Wine Routes and the recently inaugurated 'Wine Train,' which certainly constitutes a novelty. However, we cannot live in a fantasy world. There are problems to correct. In the field of promotion, I propose that we insist on the basic concept of Chile from the following perspectives:

> *"When one spends a lifetime working in the same field, such as in my case, nearly four decades in the wine business, it is very difficult to be surprised by ideas or projects that are completely original.*
>
> *Likewise, I am not original in maintaining that life is cyclical and therefore passes the same place several times. As Italian author Lampedusa very clearly said in Il Gattopardo, 'everything must change for everything to remain the same.'"*

In Chile the current trend is to promote the concept of Chile as a nation in order to better export our products in an increasingly globalized world.

It's an idea that is 'older than black thread,' which doesn't make it any less valid. Commissions have been created, studies have been conducted, strategic development plans have been formulated, and Oh! What news! The conclusion is that the average person around the world knows little or nothing about Chile. In referring to this subject in the past, I have said that "French wine, good or bad, sells because it is French, while in our case, when we want to sell ourselves we have to start by explaining that Chile is not in Africa."

I propose that our presence in the world be focused not on logos or slogans, but on the word CHILE. In my opinion, despite being a synonym for hot peppers, the name of our beloved homeland (although the origin is yet to be explained), is symbol enough; it's short, easy to pronounce in almost any language, and possibly has as much impact as the Australian kangaroo.

As it happens, almost the only natural means of spreading the name is through bottled Chilean wine, which reaches the consumer with the name 'Chile' in plain view. This is obviously not the case with fruit or salmon, and certainly not with copper, cellulose, or fish meal.

If wine exporters agreed to place the word CHILE on their labels in a uniform size, location, and typography, based on the number of bottles of wine exported in 2002, would our beloved name be repeated at least 300,000,000 times per year. A simple analysis indicates that it would be virtually impossible to achieve coverage of a similar magnitude in any publicity campaign, as the cost would be prohibitive.

Once again I reiterate that Chilean wine is possibly the best thing that has ever happened to Chile. I insist that being able to produce it and successfully offer it to the world is a source of great prestige and respect.

And behind it there is culture, knowledge, and distinction, in the healthy and positive sense of the word. Repeating our name and including it in all of our graphic and audiovisual representations requires no national symbols such as the copihue (national flower) or the spurs or ponchos of the huaso (Chilean cowboy) or even the Easter Island moai.

The word CHILE alone is enough, a true national trademark to stand behind our wines, with the glory that our country deserves.

Rodrigo Alvarado

APPENDICES

WINE TIME LINE THROUGH HISTORY
APPENDIX I

70,000,000	First vines appear in Eurasia.
2,000,000	First appearance of genus *Homo, Homo habilis*.
12,000	Humans begin to select vines.
6000	*Vitis vinifera sativa* first grown in Europe and Asia.
3500	Population grows around Mediterranean and diversified agriculture begins with wheat, vines, and olives.
3000	First civilizations appear in Mesopotamia and Egypt.
2647	Foundation of the Ancient Kingdom of Egypt; irrigation systems created.
2500	Merchants from Lagash trade in wines from southern Mesopotamia.
1800	Wine and oil stored in the Palace of Knossos, Crete.
1792	Hamurabi regulates the commerce of wine in Mesopotamia.
1300	Paintings in the tomb of Amun depict Egypt's vinification systems, gathering grapes in wicker baskets, and treading grapes to break the skins. Musts ferment in clay containers and are later sealed.
1200	Phoenicians control wine trade in Mediterranean Sea.
753	Foundation of Rome, beginning of the monarchy.
750	Foundation of Greek colonies in Greater Greece and Italy. New winemaking methods spread.
400	Greek physician Hippocrates of Cos prescribed wine as disinfectant, purgative, and diuretic.
460	Euripides' Greek Tragedy, The Bacchae, where music and wine prevails.

440		Conversation flows along with a gradual consumption of wine during symposiums and banquets.
202		Rome conquers Carthage, controls Mediterranean and wine trade.
186		Roman Senate prohibits Bacchanalian rites honoring Bacchus.
51		Julius Caesar conquers Gaul. Garonne River trade route established, passing through Bordeaux. Gauls introduce Romans to advantages of wooden containers.
31	BC	Octavian accedes to power after Battle of Actium, and Empire begins.
0		Birth of Jesus in Roman province of Judea.
71	AD	First vineyards registered in Bordeaux.
79		Vesuvius buries Pompey, city of wealthy wine merchants.
395		Christianity declared official religion of the Roman Empire.
476		End of Roman Empire.
476		Medieval wineries continue wine production.
711		Moslems conquer the Iberian Peninsula and prohibit wine consumption.
800		Clay vessels (amphora and dolia) replaced by rudimentary wooden containers. Their cylindrical shape facilitated transport at the expense of wine quality.
1000		Vine growing spreads to northern and eastern Europe, especially Alsace and the north of what is today Hungary.
1000		Viking Explorations. Leif Ericsson, son of Eric the Red, explores a region he calls Vinland.

1350	Rebirth of trade. The Hanseatic League controls wine trade in the Baltic Sea.
1400	France begins to establish itself as a major wine producer.
1493	Christopher Columbus takes grape vines along on his second voyage to America and introduces the vine to the new continent.
1524	Hernán Cortés orders vineyards planted in central Mexican highlands.
1532	Portuguese Martin Alonso de Souza takes vines to St. Vincent in southern Brazil.
1548	Bartolomé de Terrazas introduces vines to Peru.
1548 Chile	Francisco de Carabantes introduces the vine to Chile.
1550 Chile	Alonso Moreno credited with first wine sale, according to José Toribio Medina.
1555 Chile	Rodrigo de Araya makes first wines in Santiago.
1557 Chile	Juan Cidrón takes vines across the Andes, from La Serena (Chile) to Santiago del Estero (Argentina).
1561	Spanish conquistador Juan Jufré founds city of San Juan and introduces vine growing to Mendoza.
1562	French settlers unsuccessfully attempt to plant vineyards in Florida.
1619	English settlers bring grape vines to Virginia.
1655	Dutch colonists plant vineyards in Cape Town, South Africa.
1657	First wine bottle created for the King's Head Tavern in Oxford.

1680		Dom Perignon creates Champagne in Hautvillers.
1776		Mission priests led by Junípero Serra obtained wine in California.
1788		British settlers plant vineyards in Farm Cove, Australia.
1810	Chile	Chile's first governing body formed and independence begins.
1819		Missionary Marsden brings grape vines to New Zealand.
1822		Birth of Louis Pasteur, whose research on pasteurization led to stability in wine.
1845	Chile	New vine varieties introduced in Chile, such as Cabernet Sauvignon, Cabernet Franc, Cot (Malbec), Merlot, Verdot, Carmenère, Sauvignon Blanc, Chardonnay, Semillon, Riesling, and Gewürztraminer.
1846		Fungal disease, later identified as Oidium (Powdery Mildew), first detected in Versailles, France.
1851	Chile	Silvestre Ochagavía introduced French and German varieties in Chile.
1853		Nathaniel Rothschild acquires Château Brane-Mouton in the Medoc region north of Bordeaux. The name is later changed to Château Mouton Rothschild.
1855		First official classification of fine Bordeaux wines. Château Lafite-Rothschild, Château Latour, Château Margaux y Château Haut-Brion are named *premiers crus*.
1855		George Yount introduces the Mission Variety in Napa Valley.
1856	Chile	Matías Cousiño acquires the Hacienda de Macul.
1860		Phylloxera attacks French vineyards, later spreading throughout the rest of the world, with the exception of Chile.

1879	Chile	Phylloxera arrives in Argentina. Chile creates a sanitary barrier.
1865	Chile	Viña San Pedro founded in the Curicó Valley, Chile.
1868		James Rothschild acquires Château Lafite in the Medoc region.
1870	Chile	Maximiano Errázuriz founds Viña Errázuriz Panquehue in the Acongacua Valley, Chile.
1878	Chile	Isidora Goyenechea inaugurates Viña Cousiño Macul (Maipo Valley, Chile), and hires distinguished French winemaker Pierre Godefroy Durand.
1880	Chile	Decauville system introduced to wineries and vineyards.
1880	Chile	Domingo Fernández Concha founds Viña Santa Rita in the Maipo Valley, Chile.
1882	Chile	Francisco Undurraga creates Viña Undurraga (Viña Santa Ana) in the Maipo Valley, Chile.
1883	Chile	Melchor Concha y Toro explores the vitivinicultural potential of Chile's Maipo Valley and founds Viña Concha y Toro.
1887	Chile	Viña La Rosa exports first Chilean wines to Europe after success in the 1873 international fair in Vienna.
1900	Chile	Chilean wine exports begin.
1902	Chile	Creation of the Alcohol Tax Administration.
1903	Chile	Viña Undurraga sends first shipment to United States.
1910	Chile	Vicuña Mackenna Catalonians manage Santiago wine distribution.
1919		Alcohol Prohibition (dry laws) passed in the United States.
1939	Chile	Alcohol Law restricts plantation of new vineyards in Chile.

1953	Chile	Foundation of National Association of Agricultural Engineers-Enologists.
1964	Chile	1-liter bottles first appear in national market.
1973		Château Mouton-Rothschild added to list of premiers crus.
1980	Chile	Miguel Torres initiates modernization process in Chilean wineries.
1982	Chile	Pablo Morandé discovers Casablanca Valley's potential as region for fine white wines.
1986	Chile	Viña Concha y Toro creates its first Don Melchor wine.
1994	Chile	Jean Michel Boursiquot identifies Carmenère variety.
2003	Chile	Chile's participation in the world export market increases from .96% in 1990 to 5.3% in 2003.

FOUNDATION DATES OF CHILE'S MAJOR WINERIES
APPENDIX II

1850 - 1899	
Carmen	Santa Carolina
Concha y Toro	San Pedro
Correa Albano	Santa Rita
Cousiño Macul	Tarapacá ex-Zavala
Errázuriz	Undurraga
La Rosa	Valdivieso
Linderos	

1900 - 1949	
Canepa	Lomas de Cauquenes
Echeverría	Ravanal
El Aromo	Santa Helena
El Huique	De Martino
Las Pitras	Segú
Los Robles	Viu Manent

1950 - 1979	
Andesterra	Requingua
Aresti	Santa Alicia
Bisquertt	Santa Ema
Miguel Torres	Santa Mónica
Portal del Alto	Torreón de Paredes
Pueblo Antiguo	

1980 - 1989	
Casa Donoso	Odfjell Vineyards
Gillmore	Santa Emiliana
Gracia	Siegel
Los Vascos	Villard Fine Wines
Montes	

1990 - 2004	
Almaviva	Matetic
AltaCima	Misiones de Rengo
Anakena	MontGras
Antiyal	Morandé
Aquitania	Ocho Tierras
Baron Philippe de Rothschild	Pérez Cruz
Botalcura	Porta
Calina	Quebrada de Macul
Caliterra	San Diego de Puquillay
Canata	San Esteban
Cantera	Santa Laura
Carpe Diem	Seña
Casa Lapostolle	Soler
Casa Rivas	Starry Night
Casa Silva	Sur Andino (Terra Andina)
Casa Tamaya	Sutil
Casal del Gorchs	Tabalí
Casas del Bosque	Terra Andina
Casas del Toqui	Terramater
Château Los Boldos	Terranoble
Cono Sur	Terravid
El Principal	Ventisquero
Francisco de Aguirre	Veramonte
Haras de Pirque	Vía Wine Group
Huelquén	Vinos del Sur
Indómita	Viña Mar
La Playa	Viñedos Chadwick
Leyda	Viñedos del Maule
Luis Felipe Edwards	William Cole
Martínez de Salinas	William Fèvre Chile

CHILE'S VITIVINICULTURAL SOCIETIES
APPENDIX III

Of the various vitivinicultural societies that have been founded in Chile, it is worth mentioning those that are active today: Viñas de Chile, Chilevid (Association of Producers of Fine Export Wines), founded in 1993; and the Corporación Chilena del Vino (Chilean Wine Corporation), which has strictly technological objectives.

- National Association of Viticulturists, successor to the National Vitivinicultural Syndicate, founded in the early 20th century.
- Association of Wine Wholesalers, later called the Chamber of Wine.
- Association of Wine Bottlers and the Wine Exporters Consortium, which joined in 1967 to form the Chilean Association of Wine Exporters and Bottlers. The organization was renamed Viñas de Chile in 2000.
- Wine Brokers Association.
- Chilean Federation of Agricultural-Vitivinicultural Cooperatives, founded in 1967.
- Chilean Vitivinicultural Corporation, which aimed to unite all of the above, although irreconcilable differences doomed the attempt to failure.

We must also include mention of the Brotherhood of Vitivinicultural Merit, which consists of Agricultural Engineer-Enologists who have received the Vitivinicultural Merit Award, the past presidents of the Association of Agricultural Engineer-Enologists (founded in 1952), and those who have been recognized for their contributions to the development of wine. This organization was founded on December 30, 1993, as an initiative of Alejandro Hernández, who belongs to several similar institutions in Europe. The founding members were:
Rodrigo Alvarado, Ruy Barbosa (first president), Lila Carrasco, Sergio Correa, Sergio Daneri, Raúl Durand, Mario Espinoza, Mario Geisse, Alejandro Hernández, Arturo Lavín, Guillermo Machala, Emilio Merino, Ricardo Merino, Philippo Pszczólkowski, Jaime Ríos, Emilio de Solminihac, Felipe de Solminihac, Armando Vieira, and Goetz von Gersdorf.

Chilean Vitivinicultural Regions
APPENDIX IV

The May 1995 Decree Law N° 464 established Chile's wine regions, or appellation system, based on the 1985 Alcohol Law. The law was updated in May 2002 and presents a coherent and efficient legal body in accordance with the European Union's regulations concerning the potability of wine. The Decree establishes an appellation system (Denomination of Origin) that divides the country into five vitivinicultural zones, which are then further divided into sub-regions, zones, and areas. Within this scheme, wines are classified into three categories: those with denomination of origin, those without denomination of origin, and table wines.

The first category includes wines made with varieties specified in the Decree, and their origin must be shown on the label. The second category includes wines made from *Vitis vinifera* grapes without specifying origin, and the final category is limited to wines made from *Vitis vinifera sativa* table grapes.

The Decree also establishes regulations regarding the blending of wines from different regions and introduces a novel procedure: taxation is monitored through certified external enterprises supervised by the Agriculture and Livestock Service (SAG). Decree N° 464 is thereby recognized world-wide for its ability to certify the origin of a wine, the varieties used, and its vintage year based on an easily-applied process that is readily understood by consumers.

Vitivinicultural Denomination of Origin 2004
Appendix V

REGIONS	SUB-REGIONS	ZONES	AREAS	
Atacama	Copiapó Valley			
	Huasco Valley			
Coquimbo	Elqui Valley		Vicuña	
			Paiguano	
	Limarí Valley		Ovalle	Monte Patria
			Punitaqui	Río Hurtado
	Choapa Valley		Salamanca	Illapel
Aconcagua	Aconcagua Valley		Panquehue	
	Casablanca Valley			
	San Antonio Valley	Leyda Valley	San Juan	
			Marga Marga	
Central Valley	Maipo Valley		Santiago	Pirque
			Puente Alto	Buin
			Isla de Maipo	Talagante
			Melipilla	Alhué
				María Pinto
	Rapel Valley	Cachapoal Valley	Rancagua	Requínoa
			Rengo	Peumo
		Colchagua Valley	San Fernando	Chimbarongo
			Nancagua	Santa Cruz
			Palmilla	Peralillo
			Lolol	Marchigüe
	Curicó Valley	Teno Valley	Rauco	Romeral
		Lontue Valley	Molina	Sagrada Familia
	Maule Valley	Claro Valley	Talca	Pencahue
			San Clemente	San Rafael
		Loncomilla Valley	San Javier	Villa Alegre
			Parral	Linares
		Tutuvén Valley	Cauquenes	
Southern Regions	Itata Valley		Chillán	Quillón
			Portezuelo	Coelemu
	Bio Bío Valley		Yumbel	Mulchén
	Malleco Valley		Traiguén	

CHILE'S MAJOR WINERIES 2004
APPENDIX VI

WINERIES	CAPACITY Cellar (1,000)	SURFACE AREA Vineyards (hectares)	APPELLATION
Almaviva	599	42	Maipo
Altacima	838	62	Lontué
Anakena	2,080	153	Rapel
Andesterra	3,500	250	Curicó
Antiyal	17	3	Maipo
Aquitania	400	29	Maipo and Traiguén
Aresti	11,000	400	Molina
Astaburuaga	1,600	60	Sagrada Familia
Balduzzi	300	100	Maule
Barón Philippe R.	1,382	-	Maipo
Bisquertt	14,618	705	Colchagua
Calina	2,675	54	Maule
Caliterra	6,300	305	Casablanca, Maipo and Rapel
Camino Real	1,800	83	Cachapoal
Canata	3,200	300	Bío Bío
Canepa	19,375	1,000	Maipo and Rapel
Cantera	9,000	1,000	Colchagua
Carmen	9,850	520	Maipo
Carpe Diem	3,600	300	Maule and Itata
Carta Vieja	14,000	748	Maule
Casa Donoso	2,375	149	Maule
Casa Lapostolle	1,350	300	Casablanca, Colchagua and Cachapoal
Casa Marín	250	35	San Antonio
Casa Rivas	2,935	217	Maipo
Casa Silva	6,500	650	Colchagua
Casa Tamaya	1,470	108	Limarí
Casablanca	1,000	70	Casablanca and Maipo
Casal del Gorchs	1,000	100	Pirque, Apalta and Casablanca
Casas del Bosque	983	180	Casablanca and Rapel
Casas de Giner	1,821	350	Itata
Casas Patronales	1,800	280	Maule

WINERIES	CAPACITY Cellar (1,000)	SURFACE AREA Vineyards (hectares)	APPELLATION
Château Los Boldos	5,000	350	Requínoa
Chocalán	1,538	78	Maipo
Concha y Toro	168,600	1,290	Casablanca, Maipo, Rapel, Curicó and Maule
Cono Sur	8,500	680	Casablanca, Rapel, Maipo and Bío-Bío
Correa Albano	4,352	10	Curicó
Cousiño Macul	8,000	396	Maipo
Cremaschi Furlotti	7,200	160	Maule
De Larose	3,122	102	Cachapoal
De Martino	8,000	300	Maipo
Doña Javiera	1,500	50	Maipo
Echeverría	3,000	80	Molina
El Aromo	8,138	150	Maule
El Huique	1,200	100	Colchagua
El Principal	500	54	Maipo
Errázuriz	3,400	358	Aconcagua, Casablanca, Maipo and Curicó
Errázuriz Ovalle	28,000	2,591	Curicó
Estampa	1,825	260	Colchagua
Falernia	2,050	320	Elqui
Francisco de Aguirre	6,234	266	Limarí
Gillmore	400	60	Maule
Gracia	9,000	396	Aconcagua, Maipo, Rapel and Bío-Bío
Haras de Pirque	1,790	143	Pirque
Huelquén	3,000	90	Maipo
Hugo Casanova	2,000	100	Maule
Indómita	1,400	250	Casablanca, Maule and Maipo
Inés Escobar	3,800	160	Curicó and Sagrada Familia
J. Bouchon	3,500	330	Colchagua and Maule
La Fortuna	4,000	250	Lontué
La Playa	1,150	50	Colchagua and Maule
La Posada	1,000	101	Colchagua
La Ronciere	3,500	200	Cachapoal and Colchagua

WINERIES	CAPACITY Cellar (1,000)	SURFACE AREA Vineyards (hectares)	APPELLATION
La Rosa	17,000	750	Cachapoal
Las Pitras	4,500	210	Curicó
Leyda	1,340	80	San Antonio
Linderos	890	121	Maipo and Colchagua
Los Robles	20,000	1,000	Curicó
Lomas de Cauquenes	22,500	2,000	Maule
Los Vascos	11,500	630	Colchagua
Luis Felipe Edwards	5,200	292	Colchagua
Mar	1,523	15	Casablanca
Manquehue	3,000	250	Pirque and Rapel
Martínez de Salinas	800	154	Maule
Matetic	300	46	San Antonio
Miguel Torres Chile	6,300	700	Curicó
Misiones de Rengo	7,628	250	Rapel
Montes	6,600	550	Colchagua and Curicó
MontGras	6,500	500	Colchagua
Morandé	11,400	533	Casablanca, Maipo, Rapel and Maule
Ocho Tierras	-	233	Limarí
Odfjell Vineyards	1,000	85	Maipo
Pérez Cruz	1,800	140	Maipo
Porta	8,450	225	Aconcagua, Maipo, Rapel and Bío-Bío
Portal del Alto	2,435	157	Maipo, Cachapoal and Maule
Pueblo Antiguo	2,660	72	Colchagua
Quebrada de Macul	400	27	Maipo
Ravanal	3,005	133	Colchagua
Requingua	20,112	232	Curicó
San Diego de Puquillay	40	91	Colchagua
San Esteban	2,456	95	Aconcagua
San Pedro	56,460	2,272	Lontué, Maipo, Casablanca, Maule and Rapel
Santa Alicia	3,200	135	Maipo
Santa Carolina	25,000	1,526	Casablanca, Maipo, Rapel, Colchagua and Maule

WINERIES	CAPACITY Cellar (1,000)	SURFACE AREA Vineyards (hectares)	APPELLATION
Santa Ema	12,562	478	Maipo and Rapel
Santa Emiliana	529	1,494	Casablanca, Maipo and Rapel
Santa Helena	18,000	663	Colchagua
Santa Laura	400	80	Colchagua
Santa Mónica	5,900	93	Rapel
Santa Rita	90,000	2,000	Casablanca, Maipo, Rapel and Maule
Segú	4,000	300	Maule
Selentia	1,200	115	Colchagua
Seña	Errázuriz	60	Aconcagua
Siegel	2,000	600	Colchagua
Soler	1,060	29	Limarí
Sur Andino	2,600	0	Maipo, Rapel and Casablanca
Sutil	5,388	250	Colchagua and Maipo
Tabalí	1,000	150	Limarí
Tarapacá	10,724	604	Maipo and Casablanca
Terramater	6,400	449	Maipo, Curicó and Maule
Terranoble	1,960	122	Maule and Colchagua
Terravid	300	0	Maipo and Maule
Torrealba	500	70	Curicó
Torreón de Paredes	3,000	150	Cachapoal
Undurraga	20,000	1,000	Maipo and Colchagua
Valdivieso	11,575	200	Curicó
Ventisquero	23,000	1,500	Maipo, Rapel, Casablanca and Colchagua
Veramonte	6,775	404	Casablanca and Maipo
Vía Wine Group	17,000	858	Casablanca, Colchagua, Curicó and Maule
Villard Estate	900	23	Casablanca
Viñedo Chadwick	Errázuriz	15	Maipo
Viñedos del Maule	18,000	1,700	Maule
Viu Manent	4,850	250	Colchagua
William Cole	2,250	132	Casablanca
William Fevre Chile	1,000	70	Maipo

WORLD WINE
PRODUCTION AND CONSUMPTION
APPENDIX VII

COUNTRY	PRODUCTION 1,000,000 liters		SURFACE AREA 1,000 hectares		CONSUMPTION 1,000,000 liters	
	1997	2002	1997	2002	1997	2002
AMERICAS						
Chile	431	562	123	168	213	225
Argentina	1,350	1,580	205	207	1,389	1,204
United State	2,618	2,380	338	396	1,779	2,133
EUROPE						
Spain	3,322	3,608	1,127	1,100	1,534	1,400
France	5,510	5,421	878	850	3,652	3,370
Italy	5,056	4,700	880	797	3,562	3,050
Portugal	591	700	256	250	570	500
AFRICA AND OCEANIA						
South Africa	812	761	108	117	410	397
Australia	617	1,070	72	115	328	397
New Zealand	58	61	8	13	304	395

Glossary

Acetobacter: Bacteria that causes vinegar.

Aguardiente: Alcoholic beverage obtained by distilling wine or other substance.

Ampelography: Branch of science that works with the classification of different varieties of grapevines.

Arroba: A liquid measure that varies between 11.5 and 12.5 kilos, depending on the region. In Chile it is understood to mean 40 liters.

Asoleado: Chilean legislation defines the term to include wines obtained from sun-dried grapes from vineyards located south of the Maule River.

Cato the Elder (Marcus Porcius): (232 – 149 BC) Roman citizen born in Tusculum. His writings include seven books on the origins of the Roman people.

Chicha: In Chile, the term refers to a beverage obtained by the partial fermentation of grape must.

Chuico: 15-liter container used for wine in Chile in the mid-19th century.

Cortés, Hernán: (1485-1547) Spanish conquistador who conquered the Aztec city of Tenochtitlán in 1521, initiating the Spanish presence in the Americas.

Côte: French word meaning hillside and by extension the French name for the vineyards located on them.

Cumae: Roman city in Campania, 16 km west of Naples.

Diocles: (245–313 AD) Roman emperor.

Dioscorides: (40–90 AD) 1st century Greek physician who identified the viniferous vine, naming it *Oenophoros ampelos*. Linnaeus later translated the name as *Vitis vinifera sativa*, the name used today.

Domitian: (51–97 AD) Roman emperor, son of Vespasian, younger brother of and successor to Titus.

Euripides: (480-405 BC) The last of the three tragic Greek poets. Author of The Bacchae.

Foudre: Horizontal cylindrical wooden cask that holds approximately 3-4,000 liters used to age and store wine.

Fundo: Medium to large agricultural estate.

Galeno, Claudio: (131-210 AD) Greek physician and philosopher born in Pergamo.

Herodotus: (484-425 BC) Greek historian considered to be the Father of History.

Hesiod: 8th century BC Greek poet, the oldest after Homer, according to Herodotus, and author of *The Works and Days*, on agriculture and navigation.

Hippocrates: (460-377BC) Greek physician considered to be the Father of Medicine. Contemporary of Socrates and Plato.

Horace: (65-8BC) Latin poet born in Venusia and died in Rome.

Huaso: Inhabitant of rural Chile, especially those who use horses as a means of transportation; often translated as Chilean cowboy.

Huguenots: French Protestants and followers of 16th century French theologian, pastor, and reformer John Calvin.

Latifundio: Intricate Latin American agricultural system in which the landed aristocracy benefited from the labor of *inquilinos*, or peasant tenant-farmers, who lived on the land. The system was characterized by inefficient productivity and fell out of use in the 20th century.

Messina: Greek colony in northeastern Sicily originally named Zancle.

Mestizo: Term that alludes to the blend of indigenous and European ethnicities. Chile's population today is largely meztizo.

Pliny the Elder: (23-79 AD) Erudite member of the court of Vespasian and Titus; author of *Natural History*.

Quaternary: Geological period that extends from 2,000,000 BC to the present, characterized by the appearance of humans.

Satyrs: Mythical creatures said to be half man, half goat. They accompanied Dionysius and played music for him. Pan was the most famous of all satyrs.

Silenos: Genies of rivers and fountains in Greek Mythology. Silenos were followers of the cult of Dionysius and characterized by their boundless love of sensual pleasures, indolence, voluptuous song, and bacchanalian dance.

Strabo: (58 BC-25AD) 1st century Greek geographer who lived in Rome and Alexandria and traveled throughout the orient and the Roman Empire. His work *Geography* has been conserved and reached our time.

Sybaris: Ancient city on the banks of the Gulf of Tarentum, founded by the Achaeans in 720 BC. Its commerce turned it into one of the most prosperous cities of Magna Græcia, celebrated for its wealth and its inhabitants, the sybarites. It was destroyed in 510 BC.

Tertiary: Geological period from 65,000,000 BC to 2,000,000 BC, characterized by the appearance and later diversification of mammals.

Thassos Island: Greek island in the Aegean Sea, renowned in ancient times for its gold mines.

Valdivia, Pedro de: (1500-1553) Spanish conquistador who founded the city of Santiago de Chile on February 12, 1541. He was assigned the administration of the southern territory that made up the Provincial Administration of Chile.

Varro, M. Terentius: (116 – 27 BC.) Roman erudite, grammarian, writer, and author of *Rerum rusticarum*. One of the most celebrated intellectuals of his time.

Vilanoba, Arnaldo de: (1235–1311) Physician and alchemist, born in Valencia and died in Genoa. He is credited with the discovery of nitric acid, chlorohydric acid, and sulfuric acid, as well as the extraction of alcohol from wine.

Vino Pipeño: Artisanal wine made through antiquated fermentation systems that employ neither filtration or decantation and therefore contain a high degree of sediments.

INDEX

BIBLIOGRAPHY

Adams, Leon David; *The Wines of America*, Houghton Mifflin, USA 1973.

Aguinaga, Félix; *La Vitivinicultura Argentina: Evolución y Perspectivas*. Junta de Estudios Históricos. Mendoza, Argentina, 2000.

Alvarado, Rodrigo; *Sinopsis de la Vitivinicultura Chilena*. Boletín de Divulgación N° 1. Asociación Nacional de Viticultores. Santiago, 1967.

Alvarado, Rodrigo; *Perfil Vitivinícola Chileno*. Claudia Barriga, Santiago, 1982.

Alvarado, Rodrigo; *Chile, Tierra del Vino*. Ed. Asociados, Santiago, 1982.

Alvarado, Rodrigo; *Reseña Histórica de la Industria Vitivinícola Chilena. Desde el siglo XVI hasta 1996.*

Alvarado, Rodrigo; *El Mundo del Vino. Crónicas de un enólogo*. Turismo y Comunicaciones S.A., Santiago, 1997.

Alvarado, Rodrigo; *Historia del Vino Chileno por el Historiador José del Pozo. Visiones de un enólogo,* 1998.

Alvarado, Rodrigo; *Los Caminos del Vino*, Ed. Universitaria, Santiago, 1999.

Alvarado, Rodrigo and Gross, Marcelo; *Análisis Crítico de la Vitivinicultura Chilena*. Fundación Chile, Santiago, 1983.

Arancibia, Patricia and Yávar, Aldo; *La Agronomía en la Agricultura Chilena*. Regional Office of the FAO for Latin American and the Caribbean. Santiago, 1994.

Austin, Gregory; *Perspectives on the History of Psychoactive Substance Use*, USA, 1978.

Aylwin, M; Bascuñan, C; Correa, S; Gazmuri, C; Serrano, S; Tagle, M; *Historia del Siglo XX Chileno*, Sudamericana, Santiago, 2001.

Barrow, Reginald H.; *Los Romanos*, Fondo Cultura Económica, México, 1987.

Berg, HW and Amerine, Maynard; *The Technology of Wine Making, The Avi Plublishing Company*, Inc., Westport CT, 1980.

Cass, Bruce (ed); *The Oxford Companion of The Wine of North America;* USA, Oxford University Press, 2000.

Coates, Clive (MW); *An Encyclopedia of the Wines and Domaines of France*, Cassel & Co, 2000.

Columella, Lucius Junius Moderatus; *De los trabajos del Campo*, Ed. Siglo XXI, Madrid, 1988.

Comité Inversiones Extranjeras; *Boletín Informativo*, Santiago, 2000.

Chafetz, Morris and Chafetz, Marion; *Los Efectos Saludables del Alcohol*, Martínez Roca, Barcelona, 1997.

Del Pozo, Jose; *Historia del Vino Chileno*, Universitaria, Santiago, 1998.

Dirección General de Impuestos Internos; *Ley de Alcoholes, Bebidas Alcohólicas y Vinagres,* Nº 17,105, 1969.

Duby, Georges; *Año 1000, Año 2000, Las Huellas de Nuestros Miedos*, Andrés Bello, Santiago, 1995.

Duijker, Hubrecht; *The Wines of Chile*, Spectrum, Netherlands, 1999.

Enciclopedia Espasa Calpe; Espasa Calpe, Madrid, 1992.

Enciclopedia Salvat; Salvat, Barcelona, 1972.

Encyclopedia Britanica; Williams Publisher, 1963.

Errázuriz, Ana María; *Manual de Geografía de Chile*, Andrés Bello, Santiago, 1992.

Escohotado, Antonio; *Las Drogas. De los orígenes a la prohibición*, Alianza, Madrid, 1994.

Forrestal, Peter; *The Global Encyclopedia of Wine,* The Wine Appreciation Guild, San Francisco, 2003.

Fox, Rally; *La Mujer Medieval. Libro de las Horas Iluminado,* Mondadori, Madrid, 1987.

Gay, Claudio; *Agricultura Chilena*, Vol II, Carlos Cruz, Santiago, 1974.

Gómez, Sergio and Echeñique, Jorge; *La Agricultura chilena. Las dos caras de la modernización.* FLACSO, Santiago, 1988.

Graham, James; *Historia Sencilla del Alcoholismo,* Grijalbo, México, 1996.

Grimberg, Carl; *Historia Universal. El Alba de la Civilización,* Daimon, Madrid, 1985.

Grimberg, Carl; *Historia Universal. La Edad Media,* Daimon, Madrid, 1985.

Hernández, Alejandro; *La Viña y el Vino,* Santiago, 1986.

Hernández, Alejandro and Contreras, Gonzalo; *Introducción al Vino de Chile,* Published with the help of Cristal Chile, Viña Santa Carolina, Viña Concha y Toro, Santiago, 1997.

Hernández, Alejandro; *Introducción al Vino de Chile,* Universidad Católica, Santiago, 2000.

Hidalgo, Luis; *La Vitivinicultura Americana y sus Vides.* Ministerio de Agricultura, Pesca y Animales, Secretaría General, Santiago, 1992.

Hollingsworth, Mary; *El Arte en la Historia del Hombre,* Serres, Barcelona, 1991.

Huizinga, Johan; *El Concepto de la Historia,* Fondo Cultura Económica, Mexico, 1963.

Instituto Geográfico Militar; *Atlas Mundial,* Santiago, 1999.

Jaeger, Werner; *Paidea: Los ideales de la Cultura Griega,* Fondo Cultura Económica, Mexico, 1997.

Johnson, Hugh; *The World Atlas of Wines,* Simon & Shuster, New York, 1994.

Le Blanc, Magdalena; *El Vino Chileno. Una Geografía Óptima,* Ocho Libros Editores, Santiago, 2000.

Larousse; *Vinos de España,* Madrid, 1998.

Leyes, Decretos; *Leyes y Reglamento sobre Impuestos a los Alcoholes,* Licores, Vinos y Cervezas, Chile, 1926.

Ley Nº 4536; *Disposiciones sobre Alcoholes y Bebidas Alcohólicas*, Chile, 1929.

Ley de Alcoholes y Bebidas Alcohólicas; DS. 114, Chile, 1938.

Maino, Hernán; *Mapa Regiones del Vino Chileno 2003*, Origo Ediciones, Santiago, 2003.

Maino, Hernán (ed); *Vinos Chilenos para el Siglo XXI*, Antártica, Santiago, 2001.

Markham, Dewey; *1855: A History of the Bordeaux Classification,* Wiley & Sons, New York, 1998.

Mathäs, Jurgen; *Vinos de Chile*, Contrapunto, Santiago, 1997.

Mearde, Atilio; *Historia de la Vitivinicultura Argentina. Reunión de la Academia Italiana de la Vid y el Vino.* Mendoza, Argentina, 1987.

Kramer, Samuel Noah; *La Historia empieza en Sumer*, Ayma, Barcelona, 1962.

Palm, Rolf; *Los Arábes, la Epopeya del Islam*, Javier Vergara, Argentina, 1980.

Priewe, Jens; *Wine. Die Neue Welt*, Ed. Zavert Saudmann, München, 1988.

Purdy, Fred; *The Gringo's Guide to Chilean Wine*, Impresos Offset, Bellavista, Santiago, 2000.

Reglamento de la Ley Nº 5.231; *Sobre Alcoholes y Bebidas Alcohólicas*, Chile, 1936.

Rojas, Manuel; *Viticultura y Vinificación*; Nacimiento, Santiago, 1950.

Rosano, Dick and Mondavi, Robert; *Wine Heritage, The Story of Italian American Vintners*, The Wine Appreciation Guild, San Francisco, 2000.

Roselló Mora, María; *5000 años de Historia*, Ramón Sopena, Barcelona, 1968.

Sagrada Biblia; *Versión directa de los primitivos*, by Mons. Juan Straubinger, Edición Barsa, 1963.

Sepúlveda, Sergio; *La Internalización Vitícola y el Cambio Espacial,* Revista Geográfica de Chile, Terra Australis, 40: 111-131, I. Geográfico Militar, Santiago de Chile, 1995.

Tercer Seminario Agronegocios, Problemas y Financiamiento del Desarrollo Tecnológico Vitivinícola. Universidad de Chile, Santiago de Chile, 1984.

Texto extendido de la Ley de Alcoholes y Bebidas Alcohólicas; Chile, 1943.

Torres, Miguel; *Manual de los Vinos de Cataluña*, Pentathlon, Madrid, 1982.

Torres, Miguel; *Los Viños de España*, Castell, Madrid, 1984.

Unwin, Tim; *El Vino y la Viña. Geografía histórica de la viticultura y el comercio del vino, Tusquets,* Barcelona, 2001.

Ureta, Fernando and Pszczólkowski, Philippo; *El Vino. Nobleza de Chile,* Kactus, Santiago, 1993.

Salvat; *Vinos y Bebidas.* La Gran Cocina, Salvat, Spain, 1985.

Sopexa; *Vinos y Espirituosos de Francia*, Le Carrousel, France, 1989.

Vallejo, Claudio; E*studio Prospectivo del Mercado del Vino en Chile.* Thesis presented to receive the title of Agricultural Engineer, School of Agronomy, Universidad Santo Tomás, Santiago, 2002.

Vidal Buzzi, Fernando; *Mendoza. Los Terruños del Sol.* Mendoza, Foix Freres S.A., 1994.

Vidal, Michel; *Histoire de la Vigne et des Vins Dans le Monde,* Ferret, Bordeaux, 2001.

Virgilio; *Eneida, Cátedra*, Madrid, 1998.

Wiesenthal, Mauricio; *Diccionario Salvat del Vino,* Salvat, Spain, 2001.